D0542429

Britain and European Cooperation Since 1945

𝔅

Historical Association Studies

General Editors: Muriel Chamberlain and H. T. Dickinson

Britain and European Cooperation Since 1945

Sean Greenwood

BLACKWELL
Oxford UK & Cambridge USA

First published 1992

Blackwell Publishers
108 Cowley Road
Oxford OX4 1JF
UK

238 Main Street
Suite 501
Cambridge, MA 02142
USA

British Library Cataloguing in Publication Data
A CIP catalogue record for this book is available from the British Library.

Library of Congress Cataloguing-in-Publication Data
Greenwood, Sean.
    Britain and European cooperation since 1945/Sean Greenwood.
      p.   cm. — (Historical Association studies)
    Includes bibliographical references and index.
    ISBN 0-631-18108-3. — ISBN 0-631-17654-3 (pbk.)
    1. European federation. 2. European Economic Community — Great Britain. I. Title. II. Series.
JN15.G74   1992
321'.04'094 — dc20   92-5921
                                                   CIP

Typeset in 10 on 12 pt Ehrhardt
by Setrite Typesetters Ltd, Hong Kong
Printed in Great Britain

This book is printed on acid-free paper.

Contents

1

Introduction: Before 1945

The gradual recognition over a period of almost fifty years that Britain's destiny lay in a cooperative association with her European neighbours has involved severe, sometimes painful, readjustments. At times it has seemed that British policymakers have been almost wilful in refusing to take this on board. Yet, Britain's recent past as one of the most influential of the modern European nation states meant that, after 1945, resistance to the view that this status was in eclipse or that future prosperity and influence was dependent on collaboration with Europe was always likely. This was all the more understandable because of the particular pattern of Britain's descent. Her economic decline in relation to other industrialized states was gradual. It was already under way at the start of this century and began seriously to undermine Britain's importance in international affairs after 1945, but was perhaps not fully recognized until the 1960s. On the other hand, her loss of Empire and her transformation from a world to a regional power was much more sudden, taking place within a space of twenty-five years. The dual nature of a decline which was on the one hand, so slow as to be almost imperceptible, and on the other, so swift as to baffle reaction, had the advantage of minimizing political or social upheaval. Less happily, it also allowed an illusion to persist that a root-and-branch reappraisal of Britain's position in the world was unnecessary.

Even as her reduced circumstances became more perceptible during and after the Second World War, those on the Continent who offered partnership were politely rebuffed because, from the British perspective, her neighbours appeared distinctly more disadvantaged than she. Moreover, the price often demanded for this collaboration was a pooling of sovereignty which, inevitably, implied a reduction in Britain's own. It is not surprising, therefore, that as the sense of ebbing power accelerated, a search began for a base which would allow an essentially unaltered Britain to continue to play a significant world role. With rare exceptions, the view was that this foundation was to be found elsewhere than in Europe. Alternative contenders were an association with the Commonwealth and a 'special relationship' with the United States. These themes – the reluctance to accept that her former place in the world had vanished forever, and the persisting appeal of the Commonwealth and, more so, the United States as props to this subsidence of power – recur throughout this book.

Particular emphasis has been given to events prior to British entry into the European Community in 1973. This seems appropriate because the thirty-year rule governing the release of official papers has led to important reassessments of the attitudes of the key players and their stance on European cooperation, and of the factors which made them act in the way they did. This is especially the case with Ernest Bevin and Anthony Eden, both of whom were less dismissively negative over European integration than was once assumed. On a more general level, the rationale either for abandoning Britain's own cooperative plans for Europe or rejecting those which arose elsewhere in the fifteen years which followed the war sprang less from a determined myopia than from quite rational calculations of existing British circumstances and interests. Though much may be divined from the available evidence for the later period, the pressures and advice which caused Macmillan, Heath, Wilson, Callaghan and Thatcher to take the steps they did are not, as yet, open to such detailed scrutiny.

It was not until after 1945 that proposals for the economic and political union of Europe gathered the momentum which was to produce the European Community, but modest and disparate sugges- tions for European unity had already appeared on the political agenda, and the central threads in the move towards integration may be clearly seen in the years between the two World Wars. These were: attempts to find a permanent solution to the destructive competition between France and Germany; an impulse to create an economic bloc which might match the economic strength of the United States; and a desire, based largely on sentiment and idealism, to push beyond the confines of the potentially aggressive nation state to bring together in a federation all that through geography, history, tradition and culture might be called 'European'.

Even before the treaties which formally concluded the First World War had been signed, the French had begun to explore the possibility of integrating their own coal and iron industries with those of Germany. The motive was fiercely realistic — they wished to see a German economic recovery which would give France reparation for war damage but which, at the same time, would be a recovery which France could control. Continuing mutual suspicion between these two powers ensured the failure of these initiatives. Apprehensions which centred on the United States, rather than on Germany, however, tended to bear more fruit. In 1926, for example, steel magnates from France, Germany, Belgium and Luxembourg agreed to limit production in order to increase profitability. A year later the Austrians, Czechs and Hungarians joined the scheme. The determination to compete more effectively with the towering economy of the United States gave this cartel a distinctly anti-American tinge and even fuelled some concern in Washington that this was a first step to an 'Economic United States of Europe' (Stirk, 1989, p. 16).

A combination of these two impulses — the desire to contain Germany and to meet the challenge of American economic rivalry — can be seen in the call of the French statesman, Aristide Briand, in September 1929 for 'some kind of federal bond' between the European states. This was to be the most dramatic initiative of its kind until the Schuman Plan of the 1950s. Though separated by twenty years, both proposals shared the aims of merging elements of the European economies in order to eliminate friction between Germany and France — of particular urgency for Briand as the major treaty restrictions upon Germany began to slip away — and of enhancing the economic competitiveness of Europe. Announced as it was a month before the Wall Street Crash, the Briand Plan proved to have unfortunate timing and came to nothing. The slump of the 1930s meant a reduction in momentum for all such forms of integration, though it is arguable that European cooperation foundered in the 1920s and 1930s not so much because the times were troubled — as most surely they were — but because no catastrophe occurred of sufficient magnitude to shake a general faith in the nation state.

Given such limited progress on a practical level, visionary approaches to integration which usually had little leverage beyond their advocate's modestly circulated writings were clearly at a distinct disadvantage. Yet they existed in surprising numbers — in Holland, Germany, France and elsewhere — bonded by a mutual concern over the dislocation caused by the common European nightmare of 1914–18 and by a call for some form of integration or federation as an antidote

3

to European decline. By far the most industrious of these visionaries was Count Richard Coudenhove-Kalergi. His variegated ancestry provided him with the money and contacts to form a movement in the mid-1920s, Pan-Europe. Primarily based on a plea for Europeans to come together for peaceable purposes, plus some additional economic trappings, this organization had little to offer in terms of constructive steps towards this noble, yet imprecise, goal, and it seems not unfair to suggest that had he never written a word the history of integration would not have been altered in the slightest. Having said this, Coudenhove-Kalergi mixed intimately with the political luminaries of his day, including Briand, and something of his enthusiasm may have rubbed off onto them.

How did Britain fit into this pattern? Like the continental Powers, she followed her own national interests. These, forged by her unique historical experience and her geographical situation, were rather different from those of any of her European neighbours. As the pioneer of industrialization which made her the world's pre-eminent trading nation and the possessor of the largest empire ever seen, Britain's concerns were global. The mere twenty miles of water which separate the British Isles from continental Europe understate the physical and psychological barrier which the Channel provides. Resistant to foreign invasion, the British, for much of their modern history, faced seaward with their backs to Europe. The notion of European unity, to them, implied a union imposed by force of arms. Moreover, attempts at conquest were usually inspired by creeds such as Catholicism, Jacobinism and nationalism which seemed alien and threatening to Britain's non-ideological and individualistic traditions. Only when continued isolation seemed perilous to their interests did the British intervene and play their part in reasserting what became known as 'the balance of power' in Europe.

By the inter-war period, however, many of the certainties on which this world view was based had already begun to evaporate. The United States had emerged from the First World War as the greatest economic power in the world. Increasingly, Britain's trade operated within the confines of her Empire rather than throughout the world. Moreover, nationalism threw doubts upon the cohesiveness of Empire which had supposedly been enhanced by the shared experience of 1914–18. Certainly, support for the motherland from the Dominions in future wars could not be taken for granted. At the same time, the responsibility, and potentially crippling cost, for the defence of this vast edifice remained Britain's.

4

But these were tremors, not a cataclysm, and did little to prompt any severe reassessment towards new realities. Thus, French proposals to integrate Franco-German iron and coal concerns in the early 1920s were viewed with ancient suspicions in London and allowed to wither on the vine. 'Aloofness' from Europe was the preferred course. 'A selfish policy perhaps,' the Secretary to the Cabinet admitted, 'but the cheapest and best for our own people' (Trachtenberg, 1980, p. 191). Coudenhove-Kalergi's Pan-European ideas were swept aside in the Foreign Office as 'fantastic' and 'thoroughly impractical' (Boyce, 1989, p. 66). A similarly dismissive attitude coloured the reception of the more substantial Briand Plan, though objections to it were wrapped in more diplomatic phraseology.

Attempts by European industrialists in the mid-1920s to form cartels in order to compete more equally with the American economy were taken more seriously, especially by British businessmen. Boyce argues that by the end of that decade 'British interest in American industrial development amounted almost to a fixation; if anything, more intense than Europe's preoccupation with the "American challenge" in the 1960s or the current preoccupation throughout the western world with the Japanese "economic miracle"' (Boyce, 1989, p. 73). As a result, many leading members of the British business community, and some of the political elite, came to accept that a unified European market would be an inevitable response to this challenge. Few, however, saw this as part of Britain's destiny. Instead, fears that Britain might be isolated between the existing United States of America and a likely United States of Europe produced calls for the organization of the Empire into an exclusive economic bloc able to compete with both. It was such thinking which triumphed with the introduction of the Imperial Preference system in 1931 – though other forces also contributed to the outcome. This instinct to look to the Empire for economic salvation was to remain a compelling one, and although those apprehensions over a united Europe which emerged during the inter-war years did not create it, they do seem to have reinforced a reflex action which was to be a severe drag upon British attitudes to integration.

A key figure in the debate over European integration after 1945, Winston Churchill, was, in the 1930s, committed to the path of the extension of solidarity between Britain and her Empire. 'We have our own dream and our own task,' he wrote in 1930. 'We are with Europe but not of it. We are linked but not comprised. We are interested and associated but not absorbed' (quoted in Shlaim, 1978,

p. 17). His experience as Britain's war leader from 1940 was to reinforce this opinion and to add a significant new thread. When Europe surrendered to Nazism, Britain stood not alone as myth would have it, but with her Empire. Preservation of the Empire became Churchill's dominating concern, and increasingly this meant, for him, the forging and nurturing of a partnership between the British Empire and the United States. Virtually the whole of his thinking about the structure of the peacetime world was geared to developing this Anglo-American partnership. All else was secondary. The cluster of European governments-in-exile who, from as early as 1941, pressed upon the British Government suggestions for a federated post-war Europe under British leadership were sidetracked (Shlaim, 1978, pp. 31–40). Churchill instead urged upon Washington his proposal for a 'fraternal association' between the British Commonwealth and the United States which would include common citizenship and a common approach to foreign affairs. This emphasis on a 'special friendship' between Britain and the United States was Churchill's enduring legacy. Though not unique in his desire for this, he was its most authoritative exponent, transforming it from a vague idea in 1940 into an article of faith by 1945 and promoting it with a passion which made it appear realizeable rather than the chimera which it was.

2

Britain in the European Driving Seat, 1945–47

Britain's failure to take the lead in post-war proposals for European cooperation has been widely condemned as a lost opportunity. This, it is often argued, was due to Britain's unique historical tradition reinforced by the recent experience of war. She had stood alone and survived. Her distinctiveness had been vindicated and unlike her defeated neighbours she saw no reason to question the concept of the nation state or to seek sanctuary in some larger cooperative institution. This kind of thinking certainly accounts for the fact that, though some form of European integration had been vigorously pressed upon the Churchill coalition by European governments-in-exile from as early as 1941, the British response had been distinctly lukewarm (Shlaim, 1978, p. 33). It was an attitude which was to persist and was to play a significant part in shaping later British reactions towards integration. Recent research, however, has significantly modified this picture. Though there was little interest in schemes for European cooperation during the war, in the first two or three years after 1945 the British approach to European collaboration was far from negative and envisaged active British participation (Rothwell, 1982; Warner, 1984; Young, 1984). The question of Britain's 'missed opportunity', therefore, has to be answered not simply in terms of the deadweight of past traditions and experiences but in the context of the extra-ordinarily complex situation in which Britain found herself in the post-war period.

The key figure in this reassessment is the formidable Labour Foreign Secretary, Ernest Bevin. Until recently, Bevin has had a reputation of being fervently anti-Soviet, committedly pro-American and dismissive of the European Idea. In fact, he was none of these things. Indeed, so far as Europe was concerned, his initial stance on taking office was remarkably integrationist and embraced the idea of Britain, through close collaboration with her European neighbours, holding an intermediate and cooperative position between the two new Superpowers – a 'third force', as contemporary jargon termed it. At the centre of this vision was what Bevin called 'Western Union', an economic, commercial and defensive combination of European states under British leadership.

Although the most innovative elements of Bevin's European objectives were his own creation, the base on which he built had already been shaped by officials in the Foreign Office before he became Foreign Secretary. This foundation was the product of over a year's discussion in the Foreign Office about the possibility of creating what was called a 'Western bloc' of European powers (Rothwell, 1982, pp. 406–13). Consideration of this had arisen, in part, as a response to the pressure from the exiled governments of Norway, Holland and, especially, Belgium for Britain to put herself at the head of a new Europe at the war's end. More pragmatically, the Foreign Office viewed the bloc as a means of balancing – rather than confronting – the Soviet sphere of interest already visible in Eastern Europe and, more importantly, as a way of preventing the resurgence of German aggression should Allied proposals for a United Nations Organization be stillborn. The Western bloc proposal, therefore, had not concerned itself with political or economic collaboration but was viewed more as a multi-lateral treaty of alliance, the essential objective of which was to be the mutual defence of its participants.

Although there had been a great deal of enthusiasm in Whitehall about getting the proposed bloc off the ground, it had come to nothing by the end of the war. This was due in part to certain contradictions within Foreign Office thinking, but the greatest obstacle was the Prime Minister, Winston Churchill, who heatedly condemned the commitment to the defence of Western Europe implicit in the bloc proposal. Moreover, he was implacably opposed to any arrangement with a France led by General Charles de Gaulle, whom he had come to dislike and distrust. This was a severe impediment, given that the Foreign Office saw France playing a pivotal position in the Western bloc, and the scheme, for the time being, ran into the sand.

The Western bloc scheme was, of course, a rather limited proposal. Its emphasis upon defence makes it an antecedent of NATO rather than the European Economic Community. Yet it remains interesting for two reasons. First, it provides a glimmer of a change in attitude which the war had brought to sections of the British policymaking elite. A continental commitment, traditionally unwelcome and to be entered into, therefore, only after long heart-searching, was now under discussion as a proper and realistic element in Britain's European policy. Much more important than this, the Western bloc provided the framework for Ernest Bevin's European ideas, and it was Bevin who was to transform this narrow Foreign Office proposal into a wider project for European cooperation.

Bevin's swift and positive reaction to the Western bloc proposal on taking office is indicative of his enthusiasm for the whole notion of European cooperation. But Bevin did not simply stamp his approval upon the existing draft project; he vastly extended its scope. In three important meetings held between 10 and 17 August 1945, Bevin revealed to his own advisers and to representatives of the Treasury and the Board of Trade what has been called his 'Grand Design'. As a start, Bevin accepted the urgent need to improve relations with the French which had suffered owing to the antagonism between Churchill and de Gaulle. A successful outcome in this direction, he envisaged, would provide the circumstances for cooperation between a band of states stretching from the Aegean to the Baltic on a whole series of matters beyond merely the defensive. He emphasized that

> his long term policy was to establish close relations between this country and the countries on the Mediterranean and Atlantic fringes of Europe – e.g. more especially Greece, Italy, France, Belgium, the Netherlands, and Scandinavia. He wanted to see close association between the United Kingdom and these countries – as much in commercial and economic matters as in political questions. (quoted in Greenwood, 1984, p. 322. Public Record Office FO 371 49069)

An impetus for this would be provided by taking the control of the massive industrialized region of the Ruhr out of German hands and making the area work for the good of Europe as a whole. Britain seemed to be in a good position to initiate this as the Ruhr was in her own zone of occupied Germany. A record of one of these crucial meetings stated:

> Top Secret: the Secretary of State's long-term objective was to make the Ruhr industries a central pivot in the economy of an eventual 'Western Union'. In this way, the industries (steel and

chemicals) could be merged into the trade of the 'Western Union'. (quoted in Greenwood, 1984, p. 324. Public Record Office FO 371 45731).

'Western Union' was to remain a dominant strand in Bevin's thinking over the next three years.

Given Bevin's trade union past and his thwarted ambition to be Chancellor of the Exchequer rather than Foreign Secretary in the Labour Government, the economic emphasis which he brought to the Western bloc idea is not surprising. Clearly what he was doing was tapping a reservoir of thoughts on the connection between peace and economic prosperity and the necessity for regional economic groupings which he had championed in the twenties and thirties. This sets him in the context of a widespread resurgence of enthusiasm for a new European order which existed both in Britain and on the Continent. The motives for this, which produced a rash of organizations dedicated to some form of European unity in the years immediately after the war, were a mixture of fears and high-minded aspirations. Some, especially members of the wartime resistance to fascism, looked to a fresh start for Europe unimpeded by the type of nationalist feelings which had produced so much recent misery. Others were spurred by apprehension − of a German revival, of Soviet ambitions, of the unviability of the United Nations, of the economic preponderance of the Superpowers. Inevitably, there were differing views about the way forward. Certain French officials, of what was to become known as a 'functionalist' persuasion, were already treading the path pioneered by France in the 1920s, putting forward proposals for a Franco-German coal−steel area as a prelude to a larger economic union. Jean Monnet was among these, and a tangible inspiration was the Benelux customs union which began to operate in 1946.

There were also influential British voices calling for an imaginative policy towards Europe and especially for leadership of a European 'middle way' between Soviet communism and American capitalism. These included men of the political right such as Robert Boothby, R. A. Butler and Duff Cooper, though the most vocal champions of the notion of a 'third force' were on the left wing of the Labour Party. Bevin's 'Grand Design', indeed, had rather more in common with the views of his colleagues on the left than is sometimes recognized. The hope, for instance, of Richard Crossman, a leading spokesman of the Labour left, that Britain might 'form with the peoples of Europe a common market big enough ... to stand up to ... American

10

business' was quite at one with what Bevin had in mind (quoted in Bartlett, 1977, p. 19). Apart from the fact that Bevin had not got on well with the American leaders while at Potsdam, he sensed an American proclivity to fall back upon economic nationalism in times of recession. Britain needed, therefore, to be able to stand more on her own. As for the Soviets, he intended over the matter of 'Western Union', as on all issues between them, to pursue a 'cards on the table' approach, to convince Moscow that the European group which he aimed to construct was not an anti-Soviet instrument and to make no concrete steps forward until this had been done.

But working with the Soviet Union was to prove more difficult than Bevin assumed, and the breakdown in relations between the wartime allies was, in the long term, to swamp his cooperative plans for Europe. More immediately, though, the difficulties he had begun to experience with both his allies strengthened his desire to find a 'middle way' between them. At the end of 1945, some months after he had outlined the essence of 'Western Union' to his advisers, Bevin was speaking of his perception of a world which was dividing into 'three Monroes', a reference to the century-old declaration of a United States sphere of interest in the Americas. A Soviet 'Monroe', he said, was now emerging from the Baltic to the Pacific. Bevin's third 'Monroe', he told his officials, should be based on 'our right to maintain the security of the British Commonwealth on the same terms as other countries are maintaining theirs, and to develop, within the conception of the United Nations, good relations with our near neighbours in the same way as the United States have developed their relations on the continent of America' (quoted in Edmonds, 1986, p. 28). The attractions of this possibility were to persist. Early in 1946, Bevin spoke to the French Foreign Minister, Georges Bidault, of the possibility of Britain and France leading a Western European group which would have at its disposal a vast array of colonial possessions, suggesting that 'if our two empires were coordinated we had together the greatest mass of manpower in the world' (Rothwell, 1982, p. 422). A year on from this, in September 1947, he repeated the same view to the French Prime Minister, Paul Ramadier, suggesting that this would allow Western Europe to be an equal to the Superpowers. As Manderson-Jones has pointed out, Bevin 'perceived a world divided into three spheres of influence – the Western hemisphere, the Soviet sphere and what he termed "the middle of the planet" where Western European influence and control would be paramount. The drawing together of the Western European countries and their interests within the last sphere towards the formation of a powerful Euro-centric system, so called Western Union, was the ultimate conception of Bevin's foreign policy' (Manderson-Jones, 1972, p. 22).

Clearly, during this short period Bevin's thoughts were developing in quite significant directions. By contrast, attempts actually to initiate a new European system were sporadic. It was not until a year after the 'Grand Design' had first been spelled out in the Foreign Office that Bevin pressed his officials, in August 1946, to prepare a Cabinet Paper on a proposed Western European customs union. A month later, following a suggestion from Bidault that there should be greater coordination between the Anglo-French economies, a Franco-British 'Economic Committee' to rationalize commercial competition between the two economies was set up. It was not much, but it was a beginning. However, it was not until January 1947 that Bevin's paper finally came before the Cabinet. This stressed the need to develop even closer economic ties with France as an overture to tighter economic and political bonds with Western Europe as a whole. It never happened. And though, as we shall see, the 'Grand Design' was yet to have its final flowering a year later, in Bevin's famous 'Western Union' speech of January 1948, nothing much was done, in the meantime, to provide closer economic bonds with France. Moreover, approaches from the Belgians and Dutch for a more integrated approach were politely, but firmly, rebuffed.

How is this mixture of fervent exposition and lack of achievement to be explained? An obvious possibility is that Bevin was never fully serious about European integration and that the 'Grand Design' was little more than the impractical pipe-dream of a dilettante in foreign affairs. Against this, however, must be set the undoubted enthusiasm which coloured his pronouncements on collaboration and his tenacity – often in the face of severe opposition from other government departments – toward the idea of cooperation from August 1945 through to 1948. It overlooks too the interest which he had displayed in such schemes since the 1920s. If there is an element of truth in this explanation it lies in Bevin's inexperience as Foreign Secretary, which sometimes blinded him to what was realistically attainable in the complex post-war world in which he had to work. Indeed, it was the impact of a series of interlocking difficulties, rather than a failure of will, which really hampered Bevin's progress. These were threefold: 1) Britain's relations with her allies at a time when the wartime partnership was beginning to dissolve; 2) difficulties with France and

3) the fundamental problem of Britain's economic weakness. Each presented Bevin with a tangle of overlapping problems which worked against any easy implementation of his European projects. In order, therefore, fully to understand the failure of the 'Grand Design' they need to be discussed in detail.

1 *Relations with the Superpowers* Bevin was particularly anxious not to feed Soviet suspicions that his 'Western Union', which he intended partly as an instrument of defence against a revived Germany, was aimed at the USSR. In August 1945 he made it clear to his officials that 'he did not wish to take any active steps towards the conclusion of a Franco-British alliance or the formation of a Western group until he had more time to consider possible Russian reactions' (quoted in Greenwood, 1984, p. 325).

The Soviet response turned out to be equivocal. Molotov, the Soviet Foreign Minister, gave guarded approval when some form of European grouping was put to him by Bevin the following month. Nevertheless, a fierce campaign was waged against it in the Soviet press, and because Bevin counted Big Three cooperation as the more important objective, he applied a partial brake upon Western European developments. In the light of this, his intention now was to clinch an Anglo-French treaty and then, at a future date, informally associate the smaller Western European states with it. For this reason, the British, as one official put it, had to 'choke off' the (sometimes impatient) overtures from the Belgians and the Dutch (quoted in Rothwell, 1982, p. 417).

During 1946, however, relations with the Soviets, for a variety of reasons, deteriorated with an alarming rapidity. What was more, this deterioration was also accompanied by an estrangement between London and Washington, the product of a mutual mistrust between the two Western governments (Greenwood, 1984, p. 326). Britain's growing alienation from both her wartime partners seems to have given an intensity to Bevin's European ambitions and it was in this changing context that he began to refer to the emergence of 'three Monroes', suggesting a search for a solution to Britain's world role should Big Three cooperation finally break down. In the end, Bevin's failure to clinch the British 'Monroe' before the wartime partnership actually disintegrated severely restricted any hopes of an independent world position for Britain as she was too weak to act alone. The eventual outcome – though this was not to occur for at least another two years – was that Britain was pushed into the American camp in the developing Cold War. In the meantime, this inability to secure a European consolidation under British leadership owed much to difficulties with the French.

2 *Difficulties with France* A clear and constant theme in ideas for European collaboration which emerged in Britain at the end of the war was that French participation was essential. The final composition of any group or union remained open to discussion – the earlier Foreign Office scheme was confined to the states of north-western Europe; Bevin's ranged from Greece to Norway taking in what he called the 'crust of Europe' – but no one denied that French involvement would be indispensable. This, however, was easier said than done, and British attempts to secure this fundamental prerequisite to a wider European group proved to be a frustrating exercise.

Churchill had not been entirely wrong in stressing General de Gaulle's capacity for obstruction. Since becoming head of a French Provisional Government in August 1944 the General had gone out of his way to assert French independence. Though he claimed to be interested in signing an Anglo-French treaty, de Gaulle, to the great annoyance of the British, laid down wide-ranging conditions which he insisted be met prior to any alliance. By far the most serious of these related to a defeated Germany. Britain, the General insisted, must support the French claim for permanent control of the Rhineland and for the creation of the region around the Ruhr industrial complex as an independent German state under international control. This situation had not changed by the time the Labour Government had come to power in mid-1945. As already shown, Bevin decided to concentrate on the Franco-British link as a means of allaying Soviet suspicions. But only dismal progress was possible in the face of de Gaulle's preconditions.

To the astonishment of all, on 20 January 1946, de Gaulle announced that he was resigning as President. This, perhaps surprisingly, was not a source of joy in London. Instead it brought to the surface apprehensions which had been circulating for some time concerning the political stability of France. A recent general election had made the Communist Party the largest in the National Assembly. The intentions of the Communists were unknown and certainly worrying to Whitehall, which now saw the advantages of a strong man like de Gaulle who had kept the French political system together by getting the other major parties to work with the Communists. This pillar had now gone and lurid premonitions circulated of a Moscow-inspired Communist coup, of right-wing Gaullist resistance and a descent into a bloody internal conflict. Bevin was himself caught up in this pessimism. 'Looks like civil war within a year,' he predicted. '. . . But de Gaulle will fail, the Channel ports will virtually be in Russian hands and this is a great worry' (quoted in Greenwood, 1983, p. 50).

The predicted catastrophe failed to occur. Nevertheless the incident had badly shaken British faith in France as a reliable partner. With a powerful Communist Party playing a key role in government the danger remained that France might drift inexorably into the Soviet orbit. Added to this, the new government was as insistent as de Gaulle had been that there should be no Anglo-French alliance until Britain had accepted the French position on the settlement with post-war Germany.

This might not have been an insurmountable hurdle. Bevin initially had some sympathy with the French position. At this stage he was much more concerned about a danger to peace coming from a revived Germany than from Soviet ambitions, and he was therefore inclined towards a tough approach to the defeated Germans. Also, the French demand for an independent, internationally controlled Ruhr fitted in neatly with his idea that this region should become 'a central pivot in the economy of an eventual "Western Union"'. For these reasons he was at first inclined to favour a separate Ruhr republic. But by the early part of 1946 he had changed his mind and accepted that the Ruhr must remain a part of Germany, though its industries, he believed, should be run by a consortium of interested states. This change in policy was taken knowing full well that it would make a treaty with the French, and therefore 'Western Union', harder to obtain. The political precariousness of France certainly influenced this decision, as did worries about Soviet motives for tightening controls in the eastern zone of Germany. But Bevin's primary concern by now as that if the Ruhr were divorced from Germany the economic dilapidation of the British zone in Germany would slide into chaos. Given that Britain was already pumping food and dollars into the zone at an enormous rate in order to prop it up, the economic price not only to Germany but to Britain herself was unacceptable (Greenwood, 1986, pp. 203–5).

3   *Britain's economic weakness*   In the long run, it was Britain's economic decline which, more than any other factor, induced that severe reassessment of her world role that was eventually to edge Britain

into Europe. The First World War had accelerated a process which, we can now clearly see, had already begun. The Second War pushed Britain further along the downward spiral. Enormous debts had been run up in order to fight the war; markets had been lost and investments liquidated. The sudden cutting off of Lend-Lease in August 1945 brought home just how much Britain was dependent upon the support of the United States. A loan from the Americans which was success-fully negotiated over the following months underlined this slowly dawning realization. But adjustment to this reality was still decades away and many in 1945 viewed the situation as merely a temporary setback rather than the permanent shift of economic power that it was. After all, the experience of war had brought streamlining and modernization to certain sectors of the economy. These benefits, it was thought, could be extended under those controls which had been introduced to ensure a smooth and healthy post-war reconstruction. Exports could be expected to recover, as they were already showing signs of doing in the first months after the war.

Bevin could be counted among such optimists and this probably underpinned his enthusiasm for a British initiative in creating a customs union in Western Europe. But it was not a position shared by all those he needed to convince. While he had little difficulty in carrying his own staff in the Foreign Office along with him, from the very outset he met with stiff resistance from experts in the Treasury and at the Board of Trade. On every occasion when Bevin actively tried to get the customs union rolling, the economic departments kicked it into touch. Their objections were that the Americans, who were opposed to regional economic arrangements, would be offended, that trade with the Commonwealth might be injured and that, anyway, economic integration with the dislocated French economy held no advantage. These were to become familiar arguments and were a source of frustration to those who shared something like Bevin's vision. As Duff Cooper, British Ambassador in Paris at this time and a convinced integrationist, put it, 'the mere words "customs union" produce a shudder in the Treasury and nausea in the Board of Trade' (Public Record Office FO 371 Z10270/25/17). Certainly, the views of the economic experts appear pedestrian and cautious alongside Bevin's. Having said this, Bevin does seem to have been slow to grasp the depth of Britain's economic problems, which he initially viewed as merely short-term. Eventually he was disabused of this, and Britain's lack of economic muscle was to provide a major and irritating obstacle to his European schemes. In the end, it was to be views akin to those of the economic departments which were to dominate British attitudes towards Europe for the next two decades and it was Bevin's vision which was to succumb to more pressing concerns. This, however, is to push too far ahead. Over the next two years, Bevin, in the absence of a firm European ally, without the resources to stand alone and faced with an increasingly dangerous-looking Soviet Union, was to find himself sucked further into the Cold War as the partner of the United States. Yet, even as what now appear to be the bricks of an American-dominated defensive system were being set in place, his preference for a 'middle way' for Europe remained.

3

British Momentum Lost, I: US Initiatives, 1947—49

The years 1947 to 1949 were a watershed in Britain's approach to European cooperation. The creation of the North Atlantic Treaty Organization (NATO) at the end of this period clearly provides an example of the beginnings of a particular kind of collaboration, on the traditional military/strategic level, and is frequently viewed as the spectacular climax to a single-minded effort on Bevin's part since 1945 to persuade the United States to commit itself to the defence of Western Europe. To those with integrationist sympathies, on the other hand, these years seem depressingly negative, with Britain failing, out of a narrow-minded parochialism, to give a lead to wider forms of cooperation and hindering those, usually the French or the Belgians, who sought to do so.

There is, on the surface, a compelling simplicity to the main events of these years. With his eye on enticing the United States out of the short-sighted comforts of neo-isolationism to help defend Western Europe from communism, Bevin, it is said, tried alternately to highlight the Soviet menace and demonstrate to the Americans that the Western Europeans were themselves sufficiently self-organized to be worth defending. If we take, for instance, the Anglo-French Treaty of Dunkirk signed in March 1947, it can appear, with hindsight, as the first stage in the deliberate creation of the anti-Soviet defensive system which began to emerge two years later in the shape of the North Atlantic Pact. The purposefulness in this seems all the more evident when these two treaties are linked with the intervening Brussels Pact of 1948. Thus the pattern appears: Dunkirk 1947 (Britain and France); Brussels 1948 (Britain, France, Benelux); NATO

1949 (Britain, France, Benelux, Italy, Denmark, Norway, Portugal, Iceland, Canada and the USA).

As so often, however, the reality was more complex, and closer examination of Bevin's motives at this time reveals not only a less sure-footed control of events, but a continuing preference for European rather than Atlanticist solutions to the difficulties which faced Western Europe. This remained the case even as international affairs deteriorated. On 12 March 1947 President Harry S. Truman dramatically announced that it was the intention of the United States to provide support for both Greece and Turkey in the face of an apparent threat to both from the Soviet Union. The President went on to pledge general support to 'free peoples who are resisting attempted subjugation by armed minorities or by outside pressures'. The Truman Doctrine, the first real shot in the Cold War, was followed in June by American Secretary of State George Marshall's offer of financial aid to Europe.

These two events signified the more threatening context in which East–West relations were now being conducted, and they were bound to have implications for Bevin's European ideas. The Soviet Union's rejection of Marshall Aid and therefore of participation in what became known as the European Recovery Programme (ERP) institutionalized the split in Europe and rapidly turned Britain's potential partners in the 'Grand Design' into frontline states in the Cold War. At the same time Bevin was now released from his self-imposed obligation to keep Soviet susceptibilities in mind before pressing for cooperative developments in Europe. More than this, the United States, which until very recently had looked with deep suspicion upon schemes for European integration, specifically made assistance conditional upon a common, coordinated programme which would preserve Europe from communism and provide new markets for American business. The attraction of the ERP, from the American point of view, was that it would submerge the danger of a revived Germany within an integrated Europe, would terminate a potentially limitless requirement on America to prop up the German economy and, at the same time, 'buy off' the French, who were reluctant to see a revived Germany in any form. The *New York Times* caught the spirit of the Secretary of State's address, if not its precise terminology, when it headlined, 'Marshall Pleads for European Unity' (quoted in Rappaport, 1981, p. 126).

The Truman Doctrine was viewed without much enthusiasm in London, where officials condemned its 'flat-footed Red Bogey approach' which had been presented to the world in a 'quite lamentable' manner (quoted in Rothwell, 1982, p. 436). The Marshall proposal was another matter. This was seized upon by Bevin, who galvanized the French into a joint response. He was fully prepared to bring the Russians into these discussions but seems not to have been unhappy when they walked out of the preparatory meeting held with the British and French in Paris in July.

Because its benefits ultimately went to the states of Western Europe rather than to Europe as a whole, the ERP was to play a significant role in the division of the world into Eastern and Western spheres. Evidence suggests that this was the American intention all along. This was not, however, what Bevin wanted and he was not inclined to join the United States in a confrontational posture towards the Soviet Union. Indeed, it is in the eighteen months which followed the Marshall speech that Bevin fleshed out his European ideas, and it is during this period that he worked most actively to make them a reality. Of course he was alert to the danger from Moscow and naturally he saw it as vital that Britain should benefit from the aid which Marshall now proffered, but the latter stimulated his thoughts on economic rather than military developments and reinforced his inclination towards seeking European rather than Atlanticist solutions.

In June 1947, American Under-Secretary of State William L. Clayton visited London to spell out the integrationist implications of the ERP to the British. Here he came up against, and resisted, a spirited British claim to be not 'just another European country' but deserving of individual treatment which would permit her to be the channel for dollar aid — a partner in the process rather then merely a recipient (Bullock, 1983, pp. 413–17). When the Western Europeans met in Paris in July — following the departure of Russia and her satellites — to concert their requests for aid, their executive organ, the Committee of European Economic Cooperation (CEEC), subverted American pressure for them to lay down strategies for integration or to set up a supranational organization which would oversee the process (Milward, 1987, p. 89).

This subversion is usually laid at Bevin's door and taken as clear evidence of his distaste for European integration. But this is to see these events out of context. In Bevin's plea to Clayton that Britain should not be 'lumped in' with the other European countries, national pride was mixed with nagging doubts over a survival of American isolationism and the inability, therefore, of the US to follow a European policy with any consistency (Rothwell, 1982, pp. 434–5). If Western Europe was going to be organized, better to do so independently of the Americans and under British leadership. Noticeable here too, perhaps, are Bevin's qualms, to be expressed more overtly later, of moving too quickly and too formally. As for events in the CEEC, Britain was not alone in foiling American plans for a European common market but was joined in these spoiling tactics by France, who feared for the advantages US designs would bring to Germany. When the French delegation at the CEEC suggested, as an alternative, the formation of a more limited European customs union, Bevin sympathized with the French proposal but could not support it owing to severe opposition from the economic departments in Whitehall (Hogan, 1989, pp. 66–7, 109; Milward, 1987, pp. 64, 234). To view the frustration of the American designs as being merely the product of the actions of a Foreign Secretary with a low threshold of tolerance for European cooperation is, thus, scarcely tenable.

But neither was he ready to submit to American pressure – and, as one historian has put it, Bevin 'continued to push his own proposal with the tireless zeal of a man unaccustomed to defeat' (Hogan, 1989, p. 109). On 3 September 1947 he promoted the idea of British membership of a European customs union at the Trades Union Congress at Southport. He argued the same case privately to the Prime Minister, Clement Attlee, on 5 September. By the end of the month, this prodding had produced a Cabinet study group to investigate the pros and cons of a customs union which might include the colonies (Hogan, 1989, pp. 109–10; Milward, 1987, pp. 242–3). This enthusiasm is reminiscent of that surrounding Bevin's initial enunciation of his ideas for a 'Western Union' two years earlier.

Just how far-reaching his objectives had become by the end of 1947 emerges from a conversation between Bevin and the French Prime Minister, Paul Ramadier, which took place in Paris on 22 September. Here, Bevin told the French premier that Britain and France 'with their populations of 47 million and 40 million respectively and with their vast colonial possessions ... could, if they acted together, be as powerful as either the Soviet Union or the United States'. The rich source of raw materials in their colonies meant that 'if it were possible to achieve a real common front, the two countries in unison could almost immediately occupy in the world a place equivalent to that of Russia and of the United States' (quoted in Rothwell, 1982, p. 448). Some days later, he informed his Foreign Office advisers that he and Ramadier had 'the impression that the division of Europe into Eastern and Western Groups was now inevitable and it therefore became necessary to attempt to organise the Western

States into a coherent unity. The Marshall Plan offered an opportunity of making the first step in this direction by endeavouring to form a customs union.' In October, officials from several government departments were told that Bevin's aim was to create 'a stable group between the United States and Soviet Russia' to include, alongside Britain and France, Portugal, Italy, Eire and the Benelux countries (quoted in Warner, 1984, pp. 65–6).

Bevin's 'Grand Design' in August 1945 had not mentioned colonial cooperation. The extension of his earlier ideas specifically to embrace European colonial possessions, and the emergence of what have been termed Bevin's 'world third force' objectives occurred in 1947 as a response to changed circumstances. It was in that year that Bevin had to concede that the economic fragility of Western Europe would not permit the development of a 'Western Union' if this were to be attempted on the basis of the Western European economies alone. Britain's economic difficulties, judged at the end of the war to be only temporary, were understood by early 1947 to be too profound to be solved by a European customs union. A loan from the United States which had been negotiated in 1945 was running out faster than anticipated and was likely to bring British dollar requirements, vital for recovery, to crisis point. When the pound was made freely convertible against the dollar in July 1947, as the terms of the loan had stipulated, a potentially disastrous run on the pound ensued. As if all this were not bad enough, the British economy had been thrown into disarray at the start of the year by the most bitter winter weather of the century.

We should see Marshall Aid in this setting, and note that while Bevin eagerly accepted American financial help, he also remained determined to preserve Britain's political independence from the United States. The solution still seemed to lie in cooperation with Europe and, especially, between the European colonial systems. More precisely, the key increasingly appeared to be Africa. Here British and French possessions provided huge potential in terms of markets and resources and might therefore be a base for European recovery. Moreover, as recent government reports showed, Britain's colonies in Africa were sources of crucial strategic raw materials in which the United States was not self-sufficient. As Britain abandoned her commitments in Asia and the Near East throughout 1947 – in India, Palestine, Turkey and Greece – Bevin increasingly focused on Black Africa. Not the least of its attractions as a foundation for European cooperation was that the American presence there was minimal. 'African colonial resources', as a study of this question states, 'would enable Britain to give the economic lead to Europe which the Marshall Plan was threatening to prevent; they could provide an opportunity to create what Bevin had earlier termed "the vested interests" which would encourage a union of Western European states' (Kent, 1989, pp. 52–5, 62).

Bevin was encouraged by French enthusiasm for his ideas. But, revealingly, it was tension between Moscow and the West which was the spur to his next European initiative. From early 1947 the Russians began to consolidate their hold on Eastern Europe by replacing the post-war coalition governments with single party systems – a process of control which accelerated following the offer of Marshall Aid. By the end of the year only Czechoslovakia precariously survived with non-communist representation. Perhaps more worrying was the wave of Moscow-inspired strikes, aimed at disrupting American assistance to Western Europe – if not worse – which hit France and Italy during November and December. Understandably, Bevin was not optimistic about the next series of Four Power talks due to open in London on 25 November. The collapse of these talks three weeks later, amidst wrangling over the crucial question of the future of Germany, marked a turning point in East–West relations, destroying any semblance of collaboration between the former allies.

Two days after this breakdown Bevin had talks first of all, interestingly enough, with the French Foreign Minister, Georges Bidault, and only then with George Marshall. Both conversations covered similar ground. 'Our task was to save Western civilisation,' he told Bidault. 'He himself felt that we should have to come to some sort of federation in Western Europe whether of a formal or informal character.' To Marshall he spoke even more vaguely of the creation of 'a sort of spiritual federation of the West' to include the United States, Western Europe, Britain and the Commonwealth (Rothwell, 1982, pp. 442, 454). In the same vein, Bevin alerted the Cabinet in January to the need for 'a consolidation of Western Europe' which, he explained, should also include British and European colonial territories. The culmination of this activity came in a speech to the House of Commons on 22 January 1948 which brought into public view the whole notion of the 'world third force' which had been gestating for almost a year. His starting point was the Soviet threat to Western Europe which, he asserted, meant that 'the time is ripe for consolidation.' This should be done, he suggested, by extending the existing Anglo-French Treaty to include the Benelux states. But this was just the start. He emphasized that his vision involved

> the closest possible collaboration with the Commonwealth and with overseas territories, not only with British but French, Dutch, Belgian and Portuguese. These overseas territories are large primary producers . . . and their standard of life is capable of great development. They have raw materials, food and resources which can be turned to very great common advantage, both to the peoples of the territories themselves, to Europe and to the world as a whole. (quoted in Bullock, 1983, p. 520)

He christened this proposed edifice 'Western Union', the first time the term had seen the light of day since he had used it to describe the 'Grand Design' in August 1945.

Although negotiations which had already begun between the British, the French, the Dutch and the Belgians resulted in the military/defensive Brussels Treaty (including Luxembourg) on 17 March rather than the broader collaboration presaged in the Western Union speech, it should not be assumed that this was Bevin's intention all along. Indeed, the stress which the Foreign Secretary continued to give throughout February − in Cabinet, to European officials and amongst his advisers − to the more radical economic cooperation which would underpin defence arrangements suggests otherwise (Hogan, 1989, p. 115; Warner, 1984, p. 66). Nor was the Brussels Pact merely a device to draw the Americans into a larger system for the protection of Western Europe. Washington was kept closely informed, but Bevin's intention was that 'we should use US aid to gain time, but our ultimate aim should be to attain a position in which the countries of Western Europe would be independent both of the US and the Soviet Union' (quoted in Kent, 1989, p. 70). It was the Soviet-backed communist coup in Czechoslovakia early in March which galvanized the negotiators and coloured the treaty in practical, defensive drab. Even so, the military clauses remained imprecise, and in many ways the main purpose of Brussels was to stiffen anti-Communist forces in the West rather than provide practical support.

None the less, although the Brussels Treaty contained references to economic collaboration, it was the swan song of Bevin's 'third force' objectives. From here on his principal success lay in the creation of a security system which set Britain and her European neighbours firmly in the American camp. Thus, the signing of the

24

North Atlantic Treaty in April 1949, while a considerable achievement, was not the outcome of impressive foresight and dogged determination but, to an extent, an admission of failure. Bevin had never wanted a purely military system, nor had he wanted a defensive organization which made Britain dependent on the United States. Given the deepening world crisis, he had to take what he could get. NATO, of course, would sit reasonably neatly alongside other organs of European cooperation, like the Council of Europe and the Coal and Steel Community, which were beginning to emerge on the Continent. But it was not looking down the same road to the future as they. As for Bevin, his close association with the founding of NATO, his resistance to allowing the Organization for European Economic Cooperation (OEEC) − the successor to the CEEC as the administrative agency of the Marshall Plan − to become anything like a supranational body and, finally, his scepticism towards the Schuman Plan have earned him an unjustified reputation as an enemy of integration.

All this begs a number of questions. In the first place we need to settle just how important European cooperation was to Bevin and what that notion meant to him. If, as I have tried to demonstrate, a vision of European unity was central to his thinking between 1945 and 1948, why was so little achieved in this direction? Finally, why was American pressure on the Europeans to integrate unsuccessful and to what extent was this due to British resistance?

The last question is the simplest to answer. American leverage was applied with too much imprecision and too much impatience. Truman and Marshall acted as though Europe could be made the American way simply by providing the lubricant of financial aid. What they failed to take into account was, first of all, the fierce independence of the European states which even the trauma of a Second World War had failed entirely to erase. There was sharp resistance to selling their political independence for the price on offer from Washington. This was true not only of the British but equally of the French, the Swiss and the Norwegians. In addition, the diverse economic needs of the Europeans made a common response to the Marshall Plan ultimately impossible. In the end, the Western Europeans received the benefits of the ERP, more or less as the Soviet Union had demanded to receive them, on the basis of the needs of the individual recipient states. Perhaps the most that can be said of American-inspired integrationist policies was that, through the OEEC, they began to instil the habit amongst the Europeans of acting in a more coordinated way (Hogan, 1989, p. 437; Milward, 1987, p. 209). Two years after the Marshall speech the US had come to terms with this limited achievement. But American pressure for European integration did not cease. Instead it was applied with more subtlety, in different directions and with a recognition that the process towards unity would be a gradual one.

As for Bevin, the clear threads between the first revelation of the 'Grand Design' (1945), thoughts on the 'Three Monroes' (1945), pressure for a European customs union (1946−47) and his thinking on a 'world third force' based upon European colonial territories (1947−48) indicate more than a veneer of interest in cooperation. Admittedly, his ideas remained imprecise. Yet it seems certain that Bevin's views on collaboration implied eventual European unity. In those days, terms such as 'union', 'unity' and 'federation' tended to be used indiscriminately. As one authority has pointed out, the notion of a customs union suggested in the 1940s an inevitable propulsion towards political union. The historical paradigm was the nineteenth-century German *Zollverein* (Milward, 1987, p. 236). Though, for the most part, Bevin thought in terms of an evolution towards a system which did not have formal constitutions, there were also moments when he wished to hurry the process along and, in February 1948, even seemed ready to contemplate a supranational Western Union economic bank to coordinate the economic policies of the Brussels Pact states (Hogan, 1989, p. 115). If there was havering and inconsistency this had more to do with the complexity of the situation in which he was operating than with a lack of firm intention; and if there was a fundamental unreality surrounding his schemes they were, at least, imaginative alternatives to the British predicament of facing either junior partnership with the United States or a significant abdication of her world role.

Among the most relentless opponents of these ideas and a significant cause of Bevin's failure to implement them were ministers and officials in the Board of Trade and the Treasury. From mid-1945 through to 1948, whenever Bevin raised the issue of a customs union he was blocked at Cabinet level by the Chancellor of the Exchequer, Hugh Dalton, the President of the Board of Trade, Sir Stafford Cripps, and his successor Harold Wilson. The danger, as these ministries saw it, was that close economic cooperation with Europe would mean the end of British economic independence, would antagonize the Commonwealth and irritate the United States. When the Marshall Plan negotiations destroyed the validity of the latter argument the Board of Trade and Treasury concentrated on the others. This

obstruction has been justifiably condemned as short-sighted, preju-
diced and complacent (Milward, 1987, pp. 248—50). By the time
Bevin had turned his attention to European colonial cooperation,
Cripps (who by this time had replaced Dalton as Chancellor) had
become an ally, but he now faced stiff opposition from the Colonial
Office, who criticized his African schemes as exploitative (Kent,
1989, p. 64).

By the summer of 1948 Bevin had been worn down by this
resistance. His hope of organizing what he called the 'middle of the
planet' — stretching from northern Europe to southern Africa — had
been a response to the assertion that a European customs union
could not alone solve British economic difficulties. Now the cumulative
advice of the Colonial Office and other government departments
suggested that the African colonies, because of their own economic
and technological backwardness, would not do the trick either.
Although in October Bevin still seemed hopeful that if Britain 'only
pushed on and developed Africa, we could have US dependent on us,
and eating out of our hand, in four or five years', this was, by this
time, no more than wishful thinking, for Bevin was, as we shall see,
setting up his own barriers to European cooperation (quoted in Kent,
1989, p. 66).

This shift in direction away from Europe may best be seen in
Bevin's attitude to the OEEC, which was intended by the United
States not only to administer the ERP but also, via an international
secretariat with powers of supervision over individual economies, to
promote European integration. That the OEEC — set up in April
1948, one month after the Brussels Treaty — was devoid of any
supranational implications was principally Britain's doing. The resistance of other participants such as Sweden and Switzerland played its
part too, as did the perennial reluctance of the Treasury and Board
of Trade. But Bevin's preference for evolutionary development and a
suspicion of formal constitutions were also well to the fore. Crucial
too was the deteriorating international climate. In March the Soviet
blockade of Berlin and the consequent Western airlift had begun.
Lack of firm leadership in Western Europe in the face of this new
crisis depressed Bevin and reinforced his growing belief that Britain's
future lay, after all, in cooperating with America and the Commonwealth. Bartlett is surely right when he says that 'a common enemy
supplied Anglo-American relations with a positive energy which
economic ties alone would not have generated' (Bartlett, 1989, p. 81).

Faith in a 'spiritual federation' now went into sharp decline. As the new year opened, Bevin was arguing that economic collaboration with Europe was not only undesirable but dangerous, a view reinforced in April 1949 by another sterling crisis from which only the United States could provide relief. The notion of colonial cooperation was formally abandoned. An overseas territories committee had been set up in mid-1948, but under the aegis of the emasculated OEEC and not the Brussels Pact. Also, around the same time, Bevin's idea for a supranational Western Union economic bank was dropped. Henceforward, it was through the narrow clearing-house system of the OEEC rather than via any integrated 'Western Union' that matters concerning Britain's economic cooperation with Europe were to be channelled (Hogan, 1989, p. 123; Kent, 1989, p. 68; Warner, 1984, p. 67).

As these developments suggest, the obstruction of the economic departments was not in itself sufficient to scotch Bevin's European vision. Of course, they were right to conclude that a customs union would not ease Britain's economic difficulties but they failed, unlike their French counterparts, to project the value of such cooperation into a future when recovery had been achieved. Also, perhaps less than Bevin himself, they failed to see that the creation of such a union was a matter of political will. None the less, the reality of Britain's protracted economic problems, in a world of alarming political instability, had eventually to be faced; and whereas in 1945 these were judged to be transient, the disasters of 1947 and the sterling crisis in 1949 had begun to shatter such easy optimism. Although Bevin resisted economic arguments against cooperation far longer than did his Cabinet colleagues in the Treasury and Board of Trade, economic considerations were ultimately to overwhelm him.

Bevin's European ideas are more open to criticism on the grounds that, at root, they were based on old-fashioned British nationalism rather than a response to the new post-war age and that his 'interest in Europe had been related neither to functionalism, federalism nor Socialism, but to economic self-interest linked to the creation of an imperial grouping able to achieve independence from the Americans' (Kent, 1989, p. 70). Given that most forms of European-mindedness spring from such national self-interest, it may be, nevertheless, that there was an inevitability about Bevin's final acceptance of the views of the economic departments and that, notwithstanding his vision, the more obvious alternatives of sterling bloc and Commonwealth as bases for British economic strength were likely to prove persuasive in the end. His ideas on Euro-African cooperation were also founded, it might be argued, on outmoded notions of imperialist exploitation which flew in the face of a process of decolonization soon to begin. Yet this is asking Bevin to have foreseen the unpredictable; and, as Bartlett points out, 'for the British government to have embarked upon a policy of precipitate withdrawal in the later 1940s would have been widely regarded as defeatist and as a premature act of abdication entailing prospective material as well as immediate political loss' (Bartlett, 1989, p. 73). This was just what Bevin's European schemes were intended to prevent. Oddly enough, perhaps, for a man of such vigour, his actions proved fatally hesitant. Fearful, even since he had entered the Foreign Office, of Soviet antagonism and American displeasure, he had delayed to the point where opportunities for British initiatives on European cooperation had become fatally limited. In the end, it was his misfortune that the Cold War intensified before any of the major obstacles to the 'Grand Design' could be overcome; and in the face of the apparent threat from the East, military rather than economic consolidation came to dominate his policy.

4

British Momentum Lost, II: The French and the Schuman Plan, 1949–51

The collapse of Bevin's 'Grand Design' under the weight of political and economic realities was highlighted in a paper presented to the Cabinet jointly by the Foreign Secretary and the Chancellor of the Exchequer in October 1949. This emphasized the pre-eminence of Britain's relations with the Commonwealth and with the United States and asserted that 'we must remain, as we have always been in the past, different in character from other European nations and fundamentally incapable of wholehearted integration with them' (quoted in Bullock, 1983, p. 734). For the first time since Bevin had come to the Foreign Office, European cooperation was emphatically reduced to division three in the league table of British foreign policy priorities. Earlier, in March, he had agreed with a Foreign Office committee's judgement that while the promotion of Britain as a world third force might be pursued in conjunction with consolidating the West under the wing of the Americans, should 'the two policies begin to diverge this country must ... incline towards a western preponderance' (quoted in Adamthwaite, 1985, p. 229).

Indications of this retreat were there even as Bevin's schemes for economic cooperation were at their height, and during the latter part of 1948 he had devoted much energy to the emasculation of a proposal for a European parliament, or Council of Europe. His notorious dismissal of the idea – 'I don't like it. I don't like it. When you open that Pandora's Box you'll find it full of Trojan horses' – has gone down almost as an epitaph for the Foreign Secretary's supposed repugnance towards the very concept of European collaboration (quoted in Young, 1984, p. 109). Again, the reality was more complex. Because he deeply mistrusted the supranational trappings which were attached to the proposal, he clearly would have preferred that it had never arisen in the first place. Once aired, his first response was to try and make it more compatible with his own European designs.

Churchill had been the midwife of the Council of Europe. In speeches at Zurich (September 1946) and the Hague (May 1948) calling for a United States of Europe he had tapped an emotional response within many Europeans. Recognizing the essential vagueness of Churchill's exhortations, Bevin, his Cabinet colleagues and his counsellors in the Foreign Office were at first inclined to see them as a passing irrelevance. The French, however, were inspired by Churchill's statements, and, by August 1948, they had decided to press at the autumn meeting of the Brussels Pact powers for a European Assembly which, it was suggested, should ultimately have executive powers.

That a much more narrowly defined body eventually emerged was largely Bevin's doing. None the less, despite his own misgivings, he was ready to accept that a European Assembly might have a certain value − so long as it was shorn of its supranationalism. Apart from providing a general fillip to European morale, it might, he believed, help pave the way for the world third force which then still preoccupied him. It could, he thought, take over the role of organizing European economic collaboration once Marshall Aid had run out. At the lowest level, support for it would appease the French, particularly over their desire to subsume the German danger within a greater European system, and would demonstrate Britain's European credentials to the Americans, who were enthusiastic about the idea. In this frame of mind, it was Bevin who proposed that the Assembly be called the Council of Europe. It was his suggestion too that it should be sited at Strasbourg, the symbolic junction between France and Germany.

But it was Bevin's apprehensions which also ensured that, with defence matters shunted off to NATO and economic issues to the OEEC, the Council became a peripheral consultative organ rather than the executive body which European federalists desired. This was a fundamental point to Bevin and represented a crucial difference between his objectives and theirs. However remarkable his own schemes for cooperation were, at their core was the implication that Britain would join with Europe in order to lead. When, by 1949, the pooling of British economic resources with those of Western Europe no longer appeared either attractive or realistic, and therefore national self-interest could no longer be equated with broad proposals for European cooperation, he let them drop.

Added to this, Bevin's preference for gradual, evolutionary cooperative developments left him deeply suspicious of what he called 'precipitate federalism' which, so far as he was concerned, only aroused unrealistic expectations by offering simplistic solutions to European problems (Warner, 1984, p. 70). This zeal, and not his own lack of it, he insisted was the real cause of the dilution of the Council of Europe (Bullen, 1986, p. xxiv; Kent, 1989, p. 69; Young, 1984, p. 110). As he put it in another famous phrase, 'I do not think it will work if we . . . put the roof on before we have built the building,' (quoted in Young, 1984, p. 112). Almost certainly he was right. All the indications suggest that even without British foot-dragging the chances of the emergence of a responsible European parliament were slim. The vagueness of the original French proposals, which sprang as much from hasty party political considerations as from any larger European vision, gave British objections ample leverage against which even the most fervent French proponents of the proposal quickly crumpled because the very basis of how the Council was to operate had not been thought through (Young, 1984, p. 110). In any case, to single out Britain for the failure to achieve a true European Assembly in 1948 does little to explain the lack of success in this direction during the 1950s and 1960s when that apparent impediment was absent. On the other hand, Bevin's stalling tactics over the Council of Europe helped convince pro-unity Europeans that they must develop plans for integration from which Britain might have to be excluded (Loth, 1988, p. 225).

It was in this context of a diminishing British interest in Europe that the most significant of all the post-war schemes for integration emerged in May 1950. This was the Schuman Plan. Its timing was unpropitious if British participation was anticipated, for Bevin was by now warning the Cabinet against 'associating ourselves with partners in Western Europe whose political condition is unstable and whose actions may be embarrassing to us' (quoted in Edmonds, 1986, p. 190). The formation of NATO, the sterling crisis of mid-1949 and the tightening of relations between the Commonwealth states following the Colombo Conference in January 1950 reinforced the now dominant view that Britain's future lay with the United States and the Commonwealth. There was little in the Schuman Plan likely to wean Britain away from this position. The intention of its author, Jean Monnet, who was also the driving force behind the Monnet Plan for the modernization of the French economy, was to forge the coal and steel producing regions of Lorraine and the Ruhr into a single unit which would both curtail the economic freedom of action of the Germans and bind so inextricably together the production of these two crucial ingredients of militarism that war between France and Germany would be out of the question.

Britain had only a peripheral interest in this. The fear of German strength which governed so much of French foreign policy in the twentieth century was a more fitful element in British thinking. Moreover, because of a greater perceived threat further to the east, British policy since 1946 had actually been geared towards a monitored German revival. This in itself, because it seemed to the French to lack precise controls and to be shedding existing constraints against the Germans with an alarming rapidity, had sharpened apprehensions in Paris. These were not unreasonable concerns. By 1950 the Federal Republic of Germany had been created and was a member of the OEEC and of the Council of Europe. It contained the Ruhr, which had produced 40 per cent of Europe's steel before the war. Also, although the Ruhr was governed by an international authority, the Germans were about to be invited by the British and Americans to participate in this control, and the signs were that the dismantling of German industry for war reparation was about to end. With backing from the United States and from Britain, German steel production had begun to expand to a point where it seemed likely to endanger France's own domestic economic recovery as worked out by Monnet (Hogan, 1989, pp. 364–6; Milward, 1987, p. 371). Milward goes so far as to state that 'The Schuman Plan was called into existence to save the Monnet Plan' (p. 475).

Thus, for all its federalist overtones the Schuman Plan was premised, no less than Bevin's vision, on national self-interest. Of course idealism was present too. Monnet's passion for a truly integrated Europe can hardly be doubted. The Schuman Plan also held an emotional appeal to many who looked beyond its limited provisions to a federal Europe which would create a 'third force' in world politics. In many respects, of course, it was not a new idea at all but an exhumation of the schemes for Franco-German economic integration put forward by the French immediately after the First World War – and with which the young Jean Monnet had been associated. More pragmatically, it was an attempt to implement a more tightly structured version of the International Steel Cartel which had regulated European steel production during the inter-war years. From the vantage point of Paris in 1950, the German economy had to be subordinated to the French, and quickly before the new West German state had shaken off all post-war controls. The chosen method of the Schuman Plan for providing new bonds for Germany was the controlling High Authority which would act independently of the governments of participating states. It was this supranational element which was to be the sticking point for the British over what was essentially a profoundly pragmatic proposal.

This is not to say that the British would necessarily have accepted the Schuman Plan had supranationalism been absent from it. A crucial consideration was that 'in the late 'forties and early 'fifties British standards of living, British income per head, and the strength of the British economy had seemed − indeed, at that time were − greatly superior to those of most of the Continent' (Kitzinger, 1973, p. 24). As with so many other sectors of the British economy, sale of British steel to the Europeans was not significant, amounting to 5 per cent of overall steel exports. In 1950 Britain produced a third of the amount of steel produced by those six states which were to join together in the Schuman Plan, and half the amount of coal that they produced. Surrendering control over this asset, therefore, held no obvious appeal for the British, and while there was a recognition that some regulation of the European coal and steel would be beneficial to all, the French scheme seemed unnecessarily heavy-handed (Milward, 1987, p. 405). Above everything else, though the British could see the political advantages of the Schuman Plan in settling the Franco-German problem, they were not prepared to submerge any aspect of their own sovereignty to bring this about (Young, 1984, pp. 152−3). So far as the French were concerned, however, there was no way in which they could afford to dispense with the supranationality of the Plan because only this would provide a new set of restrictions on Germany. When, in an attempt to reduce their objections, Schuman hinted to the British that supranationalism might be negotiable, he was brought sharply back into line by Monnet. A special arrangement for Britain, Monnet insisted, would mean 'no common rules and no independent High Authority, but only some kind of OEEC'. And, of course, no control over Germany (quoted in Hogan, 1989, p. 369).

To abandon supranationalism might also jeopardize crucial American support for the French plan. In October 1949 Dean Acheson, US Secretary of State since January, had written to Schuman, his French counterpart, that 'our policy in Germany, and the development of a German Government which can take its place in Western Europe, depends on the assumption by your country of leadership in Europe on these problems.' What Acheson had in mind, as he had revealed earlier to American officials, was 'the earliest possible decision by the Europeans as to objectives and commitments among them on a timetable for the creation of supra-national institutions, operating on a less than unanimity basis for dealing with specific, economic, social and perhaps other problems' (quoted in Milward, 1987, pp. 391–2). This was a green light for the Schuman Plan and marked the transfer of American hopes for European integration away from Britain and towards France.

It was a shift which went entirely unnoticed in Britain. Indeed, recent Anglo-American discussions had left the British with the distinct feeling that the United States, albeit reluctantly, had accepted that wholehearted integration would be an impossibility without British support and that the future, therefore, lay in the looser European-Atlantic arrangements which had by now become settled British policy (Charlton, 1983, pp. 92–7). This was to overestimate the significance of what the British had by now a habit of calling the 'shared leadership' of the two Powers and to underestimate the Americans' determination to promote as much political and economic integration in Europe as they could (Edmonds, 1986, pp. 193–4). These misjudgements account, in part, for the shock of 9 May 1950 when the Schuman Plan was announced in London.

Even before the full details of the Plan were available to him, however, Bevin was conditioned to reject it. This was due to the circumstances in which it was revealed to him. While Britain received no foreknowledge of the Schuman Plan, Germany did. Even more irritating, Acheson, in London on the day the Plan was announced, had been given advance notice of the proposal when in Paris two days before. Though Bevin's 'towering rage' and his accusations of collusion soon subsided, damage had been done and a whiff of suspicion still remains that Washington and Paris were working hand in glove to outflank the British (Charlton, 1983, p. 97; Edmonds, 1986, p. 210). It was over a week before the French felt able to provide further details on how the Plan might actually operate. To British astonishment, these had not yet been thought out. In the meantime, tempers in London had cooled and the proposal was examined with some attempt to assess its basic merits. The initial obstacle, a sense of betrayal, now gave way, however, to a Whitehall consensus that Britain could not accept the supranational principles involved. The possibility survived, with some encouragement from Schuman, that Britain would be able to participate in the forthcoming negotiations without commitment to supranationalism. But this hope was dashed on 1 June when the French Foreign Minister proposed a European conference on the Plan which would commit participants beforehand to the creation of a supranational authority for the integrated coal and steel industries. A response was demanded within twenty-four hours.

The ultimatum appeared to the British as further evidence of French bad faith. It has been excused as a necessity in order to eliminate British delaying tactics and because 'France had the chance to pin Germany down and was not going to lose it' (Young, 1984, p. 157). Clearly the danger existed that the British might attempt to undermine the Schuman Plan as they had the Council of Europe. Cripps, for instance, spoke of wishing to 'steer' it in a direction in which Britain could approve and Bevin pondered on the possibility of directing it along a 'realistic' path (Young, 1984, pp. 152, 154; Bullen, 1986, p. 247). On the other hand, there seems to have been a recognition by the British in their discussions of the Plan that some loss of sovereignty might be tolerable given the overall benefits of the proposal. What was unacceptable was the failure of the Schuman proposal to spell out the limits to supranationalism. Nevertheless, once they had decided to reject the ultimatum, the British went out of their way not to sabotage the initiative either by publicizing counter-proposals or by working upon known opposition to the Schuman Plan inside the French government.

It is hard to avoid the conclusion that the very announcement of the proposal, as one French federalist was to suggest to Bevin, 'had been intentional to make it impossible for [the British] to come in as those responsible did not really desire [British] cooperation' (quoted in Warner, 1984, p. 73). Anglo-French jealousy was never very far from the surface. At the time of Bevin's 'Western Union' speech in January 1948 the French, resentful of Britain's assumption of the role of leader of Europe, had made a parallel, secret, proposal to Washington (Barnet, 1984, p. 128). And when, in September 1949, the British sprang the devaluation of sterling upon the French without warning, it left an impression in France that 'nobody now thought that Britain cared a damn about consultation' (Cairncross, 1985, p. 280). The French suggestions for a European parliament which were to result in the Council of Europe had been motivated, to an extent at least, by desires to grasp the initiative in Europe. 'Federalism', it has been noted, 'was a useful French weapon in saving Western Europe from the "*cauchemar d'une predominance britannique*"' (Kent, 1989, p. 69). It may be, therefore, that Monnet was prepared to exclude the British from the Schuman initiative less because Britain was a major opponent of integration and more because of her recent prominence in proposals for European cooperation. If this was the case, a Plan dressed in the visionary clothing of European unity was essentially geared to the domination of France over Germany and the exclusion of Britain from Europe.

Certainly a long process of marginalization, whether entirely self-inflicted or otherwise, had now begun, and 'its failure to respond positively to the Schuman Plan is widely regarded as the most crucial of the opportunities which the Labour government allegedly missed between 1945 and 1951' (Warner, 1984, p. 72). This holds a number of implications: that Britain did not recognize that Monnet and Schuman were offering 'an inspired answer to what the British themselves had defined as the problem of the "future place of Western Germany in Europe"' (Edmonds, 1986, p. 210); that the British did not understand the full implications for Europe of what the French were proposing; that they did grasp the import of the scheme but were anyway determined to scotch it.

The first of these is easily disposed of, and recently released documentation clarifies beyond doubt that both the Foreign Office and the Treasury accepted and supported the Franco-German implications of the Plan, and wished to be associated in discussions between the two states but were restrained from doing so because of what was regarded as the unnecessarily complicating factor of the supranational principle (Bullen, 1986, pp. 71–2).

The publication of a dismissively negative Labour Party pamphlet on the subject of 'European Unity' only a week before a conference on the Schuman Plan between France, West Germany, Italy and the Benelux countries opened in Paris on 20 June gave credence to the belief that London was bent upon a policy of obstruction. The Americans thought it 'deplorable'. To Monnet it vindicated his recent tactics. Its timing and its tone were, indeed, regrettable, though the government's embarrassment is, in itself, an indication of a desire to avoid such accusations and even to let the French go ahead if this meant a reconciliation with Germany. The statement had, anyway, been drafted months before by Denis Healey and modified only slightly in the light of the Schuman Plan. In essence, it did little more than repeat the, by now familiar, arguments against federalism: that Britain was a world Power; that she wished to maintain her links with the United States and the Commonwealth; that cooperation between the European governments was all that was necessary and that 'third force' neutralism would endanger the Atlantic alliance. Apart from this, there was no contradiction between 'European Unity' and what the British had been saying face-to-face with the French since the Schuman Plan had first been revealed to them. Underlying the British view were feelings that now that the decision had been made to concentrate on the relationship with the United States this policy could best be served outside an integrated Europe, and that, in any case, the Schuman Plan was too ambitious and would inevitably have to be toned down so as to fit in with the kind of inter-governmental cooperation that Britain was proposing.

If the British were not alive to the full potential of the Schuman-Monnet proposals they were not alone in this, for most of the French Cabinet seem to have failed to grasp all the implications (Bullock, 1983, p. 769). Doubts continued to exist for some time whether the French Chamber of Deputies would ever ratify the Plan (Bullen, 1986, p. 365). And if the British response now appears parochial we need to recall the context in which the French proposals were made. A refusal to hand over command of the coal and steel industries – the one recently nationalized, the other apparently about to be – to an authority whose limits had not been defined does not seem unreasonable. The British were, after all, obeying what might be called the First Law of European Integration: a state will only surrender to the common good if an enhancement of its own particular interests is clearly evident. So too were the French and the Germans.

The fruit of the Schuman Plan, the European Coal and Steel Community (ECSC), made up of France, West Germany, Italy and the Benelux countries coming together in the Treaty of Paris in April 1951, was functioning by early 1953. But it presented no immediate challenge to British scepticism. There was little indication that a new Europe had been born, for the organization which Monnet had anticipated would pool coal and steel resources of its members under the command of a binding High Authority was only imperfectly created. In the difficult months of negotiation preceding the Paris Treaty a series of compromises to accommodate the weaker Dutch, Belgian and Italian economies meant that there was never a pure common market, especially in steel. Also, reservations on the part of Holland and Belgium over the powers of the High Authority resulted in a Council of Ministers and a Common Assembly which permitted some exercise of governmental control.

Without a doubt the very existence of the ECSC powerfully affected the progress of European cooperation, but its most concrete political impact was not the creation of Europe but the formation of that Franco-German alliance which has coloured developments towards integration ever since. Seen in this more muted light, 'the Schuman Plan was, in a sense, a defeat for federalism and evidence that the French had learnt the impossibility of making a European constitution' (Young, 1984, p. 189). The mistake had been to hang federalist trimmings on a proposal which was far more practical then, say, that for a European parliament, which had appeared two years before. Acheson later wrote that Britain's refusal to take part in the Schuman Plan was 'the great mistake of the post-war period' (Acheson, 1969, p. 385). It is equally arguable that the 'missed opportunities' were not those of the British, but rather those of Monnet. By excluding Britain, 'the cost of Monnet's tactics was a limited Europe, of only six nations, based on bureaucratic functional lines rather than an evolving, living, political organism, covering a wide area of Europe, such as Bevin had always hoped to create' (Young, 1984, p. 166).

Superficially, the period immediately prior to the signing of the Treaty of Paris seemed to present the prospect of some change in British attitudes towards Europe. In March 1951 Bevin's ill health resulted in his replacement by Herbert Morrison at the Foreign Office. Within a month Bevin was dead. Six months on from this the ailing Labour Government itself collapsed and the ensuing General Election saw the return of the Conservatives to power. Perhaps Monnet's tactics in May/June 1950 had such a political turnabout in mind. If so, he severely misjudged not only the Europeanism of the Labour Government, but more so that of Churchill. Monnet was not alone in this.

In a Commons debate on the Schuman Plan in June 1950, the Conservative opposition had attacked the Government for its failure to take a conditional position in the negotiations like the Dutch. 'Les absents', Churchill majestically declared, 'ont toujours tort' (quoted in Edmonds, 1986, p. 212). Yet the parliamentary debate revealed no appreciable differences between the two parties on the appropiateness of the British stance. (A significant exception was Edward Heath's maiden speech attacking the Government from a federalist stance.) Even more telling was a proposal brought to the Council of Europe in August by two Conservative representatives, Harold Macmillan and David Eccles, which merely trawled the old ground of transforming the Schuman Plan into an inter-governmental rather than a supra-national project. It was, of course, rejected by the French.

These indicators of the common ground on which Conservatives and Labour stood were temporarily hidden by the massive bulk of Churchill's reputation. To his fame as the great war leader had been added, since 1945, that of the good European. His statements at Zurich and The Hague and even the 'Iron Curtain' speech at Fulton in 1946 had all contributed. So too had his role in founding a United States of Europe Movement and in the promotion of a European Assembly, and his condemnation of the Labour Government for its apparent blocking of the road to European unity. Because of Churchill's high European profile, the Conservative Party was misleadingly perceived as the Party of Europe. In reality, the return of the Conservatives to office in 1951 made not a scrap of difference to the British response to integration nor to the Schuman Plan in particular. The chance to reopen the issue was clearly available to the new Government, for the negotiations between the Six, which were to produce a diluted version of Monnet's objectives, were still taking place and the Treaty of Paris had yet to be signed. The stance of Anthony Eden, the Foreign Secretary, was, however, identical to that of Bevin and Morrison before him — while Britain was prepared to investigate the possibility of formally associating herself with the ECSC, she would not join. This was to remain the British position for the remainder of Churchill's premiership.

This apparent contrast between Churchill's statements as leader of the opposition and his inaction after returning to power has been explained in several ways. There was, it is suggested, a loss of energy on the part of a man now approaching his eightieth year. The firm opposition of Eden towards the European movement, it is said, was something the aged Prime Minister did not have the heart to oppose (Charlton, 1983, pp. 129, 135). The fact is that Churchill had never had the slightest intention that Britain should pursue an intimate relationship with the Western European states and needed little encouragement to keep to the Atlanticist path recently cleared by the Labour Government. The federalists had been misled. To an extent they had wished to be, and had coated the rather blurred statements made at Zurich and The Hague with an unjustifiably optimistic varnish.

Churchill's true position was made crystal clear to the Cabinet in November 1951 within weeks of the Conservative electoral victory. In words which Bevin would have approved, Churchill stated,

> I am not opposed to a European Federation ... provided that
> this comes about naturally and gradually. But I never thought

that Britain or the British Commonwealth should, either individually or collectively, become an integral part of a European Federation, and have never given the slightest support to the idea. (Public Record Office CAB 129/48)

This was not new, for Churchill's approach towards European cooperation had hardly altered since he had first commented on it in 1930. What had, of course, changed in the intervening twenty years was the Great Power constellation and the rise of the Soviet state as a Superpower. Monnet had suspected that the Schuman Plan had been rejected because 'Britain has no confidence that France and the other countries of Europe have the ability or even the will effectively to resist a possible Russian invasion ... Britain believes that in this conflict continental Europe will be occupied but that she herself, with America, will be able to resist and finally conquer' (quoted in Hogan, 1989, p. 369). If this was true of Bevin it was more so of Churchill, who envisioned Britain being at the heart of three overlapping circles of interest – the Commonwealth, the United States and Europe. These notional circles were not uniform in size. The European was distinctly the smallest. Though Churchill was not beyond mischievous attempts to discomfit the Labour Government over Europe (as when calling for a European Army at the Council of Europe in August 1950 in which Britain would 'play an honourable and active part'), it was, as it was for Bevin by this time, third in his league table (Charlton, 1983, p. 137).

Those who anticipated a more committed British approach to European developments now that Churchill was back in office were never to receive a public version which matched the bluntness of statements made in Cabinet. Their enlightenment was to be more piecemeal but was, in the end, no less disappointing both to federalists in Western Europe and also to a small band of self-styled pro-Europeans within the Conservative Party itself.

5

Re-taking the Initiative, 1951–55

Anthony Eden, who returned as Foreign Secretary in the Churchill Government of 1951, has generally received a bad press in most accounts of post-war European integration. He was, we are told, 'hostile' to the European idea and 'wholeheartedly against it' and, as a result, 'may have been guilty of monumental misjudgements' (Charlton, 1983, pp. 136, 14; Carlton, 1986, p. 314). Roy Jenkins, an EEC Commissioner in the 1970s, has gone so far as to assert that 'Eden more than anyone else was responsible for allowing Europe to be made without us in the crucial years from 1951 to 1956' (*The Observer*, November 1986).

Circumstantial evidence does tend to support this view. In a statement to British representatives abroad soon after returning to office, Eden spoke of his 'wish to cultivate the idea of an Atlantic Community based on the three pillars of the United States, United Kingdom (including the Commonwealth) and Continental Europe' (quoted in Rhodes James, 1986, p. 350). This, with Europe as the lowest of priorities, was identical to Churchill's image of overlapping circles and, from 1950, would not have been disputed by Bevin. Eden did not re-open the issue of the Schuman Plan, though all the Six had still not ratified their treaty of cooperation four months after the formation of the new – and supposedly pro-European – Conservative Government. Also, the new government soon showed itself resistant to mounting pressure to join a proposed European Army, with, some argue, fatal consequences to the project. Added to this was a notorious public statement by Eden at Columbia University in January 1952 asserting that, for the British, joining a European federation was 'something which we know, in our bones, we cannot do' (quoted in Rhodes James, 1986, p. 351). Most damning of all, in 1955 Eden neglected to join the members of the ECSC as they began to transform themselves into the wider European Economic Community (EEC) – 'a development comparable with that of the exclusion of the Habsburg Empire from the Zollverein in the early nineteenth century' (Bartlett, 1977, p. 140).

There is, however, another side to this picture. We may take it for granted that Eden was no federalist. And if, as one biographer suggests, he was 'repelled' by the vision of Monnet and Schuman he was in esteemed company (Rhodes James, 1986, p. 351). Bevin, whose own European credentials were not inconsiderable, had lost interest in part because of 'the hijacking of the movement for Western European unity by the federalists' (Warner, 1989, p. 481). Eden at least had had the honesty not to associate himself with Churchill's exaggerated promises while in opposition, promises which the Premier was now unwilling to honour. Even those Conservatives, such as Harold Macmillan, David Maxwell Fyfe, Robert Boothby and Duncan Sandys, who regarded themselves as better Europeans than Eden, were, in the final analysis, no more willing to adopt supranational solutions to European cooperation than was Eden, and were more deluded than he as to what might be achieved with the Six in the absence of this willingness (Young, 1985, p. 936). Here lies one specific clue to Eden's poor reputation on this issue. The subsequent condemnation of Eden's 'betrayal' by these 'pro-Europeans' was not only misconceived but owed much to personal and political antagonisms (Charlton, 1983, pp. 139–40). Also, popular mythology which crudely suggests that Britain almost wilfully 'missed the European bus' during these years demands a simple scapegoat. The post-war Labour governments are frequent candidates but collective targets are unsatisfactorily amorphous. Churchill, despite his glaringly contradictory stance, remains largely inviolable – at least so far as Conservative memoir-writers are concerned. Therefore, we are given instead a caricature of an aged, tired Prime Minister unwilling to resist 'the hostility of Eden and the Foreign Office' (Charlton, 1983, p. 136).

Admittedly, Eden's style tended to count against any bold European initiatives. The hallmark of his foreign policy was the pedestrian rather than the visionary, the perceived task being the need to meet issues head on as they arose, in as considered and professional a way as possible. He had little patience with long-term planning, which he seemed to think was inefficient and time-wasting. In this he was unlike Bevin. But what difference, one might ask, might have been made to the path of British post-war history had Eden been less routinely conscientious and rather more imaginative? The answer must be: not very much. In the first place, his 'three pillars' suggest that even had Eden been more inclined towards the broad strategic view, European schemes would still have had a rather low priority. More importantly, an examination of Bevin's European policy suggests that a quite rare leap of imagination was still necessary in the early 1950s to cut loose from a non-European tradition at a time when Britain's world status and economic stature were not detectably in terminal decline and before the rush to decolonize had begun to erode the notion of the Commonwealth as a foundation of British influence. If Eden was not up to this then neither were Bevin, Churchill nor most of Eden's later detractors in the Conservative Party.

It is not without significance that policy towards the two most important European issues with which Eden had to deal, Britain's attitude to the ECSC and the European Defence Community (EDC), were not products of his own creativity but were legacies from the previous government. There are remarkable parallels in the origins of the two. Like the Coal and Steel Community, the notion of the EDC rested on a way of finding a practical solution to French fears of a revived Germany. This was then wrapped up in federalist terminology. The idea of a European Army, the central proposition of the EDC, also seemed, as did the ECSC, to have the warm and public support of Winston Churchill when Leader of the Opposition. Of the two it was the EDC which absorbed most of Eden's time and energy. It was also, for a time, to be the main criterion upon which British, and Eden's own, commitment to Europe was to be judged. Therefore it is the EDC which will concern us first.

The signing of the North Atlantic Treaty in April 1949 had inevitably provoked the unwelcome question of whether West Germany should have the right to its own armed forces. Most Western Europeans, many of whom had had their territories cleared of Hitler's forces only five or six years earlier, preferred not to contemplate the prospect of a new *Wehrmacht* at all. Moreover, though Konrad Adenauer, the first Chancellor of the German Federal Republic, might view rearmament as a way of further reducing Allied controls and thereby developing West German sovereignty, there was little enthusiasm for it in the new Republic. On the other hand, logic argued that at a time of deepening suspicion of Soviet activities, the Germans, in the front line in a future European war, should take some responsibility for their own defence and not expect entirely to be reliant on their neighbours.

On 25 June 1950 communist North Korea invaded South Korea across the 38th Parallel, the post-war dividing line of the country. To the members of the Western Alliance the attack was judged to be Moscow-inspired and the prelude to a possible military advance by the Soviets across the similar divide in Germany. The Korean War had a profound impact upon NATO, transforming it from a more or less symbolic statement of American support for Western Europe into a full-blown military alliance involving enormous rearmament programmes on the part of its participants and extending it to include Turkey and Greece. Even more than before, the exclusion of Germany from this defensive system looked irrational, not to say extravagant. Even the French, the most vociferous opponents of a German army but with two-fifths of their own forces tied up in fighting communist guerrillas in Indo-China, now accepted that the Germans must make some contribution to European defence. A NATO solution, however, was totally unacceptable to them because the Atlantic Treaty implied equality among its participants. A possible way forward agreed between London and Paris was for the development of a paramilitary police force in Germany which would have the advantage of being able to help fend off a Soviet attack without being a fully-fledged army.

As talks along these lines proceeded, a debate took place in August in the Consultative Assembly of the Council of Europe in Strasbourg which proposed the creation of a common, integrated European Army as the solution to the problem of tying the Germans safely into an expanded defensive system. Essentially the idea was that German contingents could be merged into and controlled by such a creation. The idea was not new and had been suggested the previous year by Adenauer. There had been little response then and it is likely that few would have taken much notice of the Council of Europe debate now had not Churchill been a participant. On the third day of the debate he made his dramatic proposal 'in favour of the immediate creation of a European Army under a unified command and in which we should all bear a worthy and honourable part'. It was hardly an ambiguous statement. Even less so was the final resolution of the Assembly (in Churchill's presence) which called 'for the immediate creation of a unified European Army, under the authority of a European Minister of Defence' and which the Leader of the Opposition pressed again in the House of Commons the following month. The hopes this gave rise to amongst federalists, however, were false ones and Churchill privately admitted at a later date, 'I meant it for them, not for us' (Fursdon, 1980, pp. 75–7).

Even in the immediate term Churchill's exhortations had little practical impact and if London played them down so too did Paris. The crisis which put the question of a European Army firmly on the agenda was provoked in neither of these capitals but in Washington. At a NATO Council meeting in September, Acheson insisted that the Western Europeans take a greater share of the defence burden by accepting a German military contribution to NATO of ten divisions. Failure to reach agreement on this, the United States made clear, would mean they would feel unable to send more troops to Europe. Fearful of a revival of American isolationism, most of the Western Europeans reluctantly accepted that these demands would have to be met. Yet, despite Acheson's emphasis that he did not envisage a German army but rather German units merging into a larger integrated force, Schuman, the French representative at the Council, was 'shocked' by the implications of the proposal. His unwillingness to go any further than developing a German paramilitary police force, which the Americans rejected as inadequate, left the French isolated.

Apart from the most unwelcome spectre of a renewal of German militarism, this turn of events threatened more specific difficulties for Monnet. Only three months had elapsed since the Six had declared their intention to work together to form the Coal and Steel Community. Sensitive negotiations were under way in Paris to prepare a treaty which would bind the participants together. Agreement had not yet emerged – and would not do so for a further eight months. To Monnet's alarm, there now seemed a distinct possibility that his European plans would be smothered in their infancy. Theoretically, the ECSC was to be a partnership of equals. Yet the rearmament issue threatened to demonstrate most publicly France's mistrust of Germany, and French nationalistic objectives in wishing to pool coal and steel resources. At the same time, German self-esteem was likely to be given a fillip which might make her less inclined to submit to supranational controls. In addition, French isolation from her prospective ECSC partners in NATO might spill over to the detriment of these other developing relationships.

The EDC was born of the need to deal with this crisis. To head it off Monnet felt bound to widen the scope of the emergent European community by proposing a defensive system which would, as he put it to Schuman, 'integrate Germany into Europe by means of a broader

Schuman Plan, taking the necessary decisions within a European framework' (Fursdon, 1980, pp. 78–84). This was further than he yet wished to travel but faced with the alternatives of a gamble on expansion or the near certainty of collapse, Monnet took the bolder course. The result was the Pleven Plan, drafted by the same team which had produced the Schuman Plan, though this time named after the French Prime Minister, René Pleven.

Like its predecessor, the Pleven Plan was not entirely novel and was founded upon ideas which had been current for some time, notably Adenauer's earlier suggestion of a European Army and the Council of Europe proposal which Churchill had helped formulate. Nor was it entirely different from the American plan which had recently been aired at the NATO Council. While this, however, had envisaged an integrated force to which German divisions (made up of thousands of men) would be added, the Pleven Plan spoke of adding battalions (made up of hundreds). Moreover, the French plan did not see NATO as the foundation for this new force. Instead it specifically harked back to the earlier suggestions of a European Army, accentuating a federalist thrust by urging the necessity for a supranational European Ministry of Defence which would be linked to the coal and steel scheme already being worked out by the Six. This would ensure that German soldiers would fight in a European uniform. It was this element too which permitted the whole project encapsulated in the Pleven Plan to be christened a European Defence Community.

It is possible that Monnet saw the Pleven Plan as not much more than an expedient for extricating France, and the Schuman Plan, from a tight corner. Certainly some members of the French Government welcomed it, and the long-drawn out negotiations which would inevitably ensue, primarily as a method of putting the brakes on the whole issue of German rearmament. It is perhaps significant that Monnet himself soon lost interest in the Pleven Plan and turned his attention back to promoting the ECSC. If diversion was the main purpose of the Pleven Plan it was not unsuccessful. Though received with some scepticism when presented to the NATO Council late in October, it gave the French the appearance of being constructive over the problems of European defence rather than mere spoilers, and their continued isolation from their NATO partners was avoided.

In an odd way, however, the Plan turned out to have far more life in it than its initial reception might have suggested. To the French themselves the Pleven solution was preferable to either an independent German army or to having German contingents in NATO, though they would rather the distasteful question of German rearmament had not been raised at all. Added to this, a concern grew among many Frenchmen that a European Army might imply the loss of France's own national forces. The Dutch and the Belgians who would have gone along with a 'NATO solution' to German rearmament were troubled from the start by the loss of sovereignty implicit in the supranational European Defence Ministry of the Pleven Plan. So too were the British, whose contribution to a common army would be an important counter-balance to the Germans. At first the Americans dismissed the notion of a European Army as militarily unworkable, though this position had to be modified when it became clear that this was the only way to achieve French acceptance of a German contribution to Europe's defence. It was this change of heart which now breathed new life into the EDC project. To please the Americans, the French had half-heartedly embraced the notion of a European Army. To appease the French, the Americans now went along with it, carrying the more or less reluctant Western Europeans with them. It was on this paradox that the EDC project was now founded. As Schuman admitted some months later, 'we were taking the risk and responsibility of provoking grave, probably irremediable dissension between allies, while we were unable to prevent the step we were opposing' (quoted in Willis, 1968, p. 139).

The debate about a European Defence Community, then, had less to do with the European Idea than with defensive arrangements at a moment of crisis in the Cold War. The view of one British official, expressed much later, that the EDC 'was a gimmick for solving two very difficult, incompatible concepts. One was having Germany defend Europe, and the other was not letting them have any power' is not wholly devoid of truth (quoted in Charlton, 1983, p. 150). It was Monnet's intervention which dressed it in the colours of the European federalists. This turned out to be an enormously complicating factor. For a start, it meant that Britain would clearly feel unable to be fully involved, though the subsequent history of the EDC suggests that had supranationalism been absent British participation would have been possible. Similar misgivings existed even amongst the six European states (the same Six involved in ECSC negotiations) who, none the less, agreed to meet early in 1951 to consider the EDC proposal. It soon became clear that the sensitive and emotive issues of armies and defence were a very different matter from finding agreement on the pooling of coal and steel. Also, the haste to solve particular difficulties meant that crucial practical issues, such as how mixed-manned forces would operate and the relationships between national and integrated forces, had not been grasped by the originators of the Pleven Plan. The result was almost four full years of, at times acrimonious, debate over the EDC both within and between prospective participants and also with the increasingly irritated United States. The failure, in the end, of a European Defence Community to materialize was frustrating enough to many. More alarming to others was that the whole episode came dangerously near to destroying the very credibility of federalism (Fursdon, 1980, pp. 105–48; Loth, 1988, pp. 249–54; Willis, 1968, pp. 130–56).

The British, although they were to receive a full share of the obloquy for the failure of the EDC, were, in fact, never the central players – these were France, Germany and the United States. Moreover, the British position on the Pleven Plan was clear and consistent from the beginning. Bevin viewed it as a ploy in French domestic politics which would have little support outside France. Its supranational elements ensured that the Labour Government would not join it though both Bevin and his successor, Herbert Morrison, supported it as a possible solution to German rearmament and asserted that Britain would associate itself closely with it (Young, 1984, p. 172). Eden, when he returned to the Foreign Office in October 1951, took precisely the same position.

The difference, after October 1951, was that Churchill's statements on European unity at The Hague, Zurich and, most recently, at Strasbourg seemed to European federalists to present a bright contrast between the intentions of the Conservative Party and the apparent niggardliness of the Labour Government's achievements regarding cooperation. This was not only unfair to the Labour Government but a complete misinterpretation of Churchill's objectives. The federalists could hardly be blamed for this and their disappointment was to be severe. More puzzling were similar expectations harboured by a group of 'pro-Europeans' within the Conservative Party who should have been in a better position to sense the ambiguity in their leader's statements and to have grasped that the attitude of the Labour Government had been hardly less pro-European than their own. These 'pro-Europeans' included, among others, David Maxwell Fyfe, Home Secretary in the new Government, and Harold Macmillan, the Minister for Housing (Young, 1985, pp. 923–6). The EDC – only superficially a 'European' concept and 'no more than a device to reconcile the French to the rearmament of the Germans', as an adviser to the new Foreign Secretary was later to describe it – now,

49

ironically, became the litmus test of the Conservative Government's enthusiasm for Europe, and of Eden's in particular (Charlton, 1983, p. 163). It was not a fair test and Eden, unwittingly, fell at the first obstacle.

The circumstances for this occurred on 28 November 1951, a month after the return of the Conservatives to power. At the council of Europe in Strasbourg, Maxwell Fyfe made a public statement on the British stance towards the EDC. His emphasis on association and not participation signalled a clear continuity of policy with the previous government. On the same day at a NATO Council meeting in Rome, Eden stated that 'British units and formations would not participate in a European army, but there might be some other form of associaton' (quoted in Carlton, 1986, p. 310). The message was thus the same, though Eden's tone was sharper. The stir that this Rome statement created is clear evidence of the expectations which Churchill had aroused. The Belgian, Paul-Henri Spaak, a prominent federalist, resigned from his position as President of the Assembly of the Council of Europe as a signal of his dismay. Members of the 'pro-European' faction in the Conservative Party protested to the Prime Minister, reminding him of his own earlier pro-European statements. Maxwell Fyfe, smarting from what he considered to be 'a personal humiliation', subsequently asserted that Eden's speech 'more than any other single act, destroyed Britain's good name on the Continent' (quoted in Charlton, 1983, p. 148).

This was hyperbole. The two statements at Strasbourg and at Rome demonstrated no fundamental conflict over policy, and Maxwell Fyfe's was as poorly received by the enthusiasts for federalism as was Eden's. Indeed, Spaak's protest was aimed as much at one as at the other (Carlton, 1986, p. 309; Young, 1985, p. 929). The 'pro-European' faction in the Conservative Party which Maxwell Fyfe represented no more favoured a federal Europe with supranational institutions than did Eden. Rather they wished to mend those fences with the Europeans which they unfairly blamed the Labour Government for having allowed to fall into disrepair and to set up a non-federal system of cooperation under British leadership – which Eden and the Foreign Office knew had been vainly attempted under Labour. Nevertheless, though the image persists of Bevin having little interest in European cooperation and Eden presiding over a betrayal of Churchillian promises, the differences between the views of the 'pro-European' Conservatives and those of the Foreign Secretary and his predecessor were largely illusory. Churchill himself, the individual most responsible for the furore, now backtracked with equanimity and without remorse. The protests of the 'pro-Europeans' in his Party were largely ignored. Indeed, it was on the day following the controversial Strasbourg and Rome speeches that he circulated to Cabinet his own views on European cooperation which unequivocally stated that 'I have never thought that Britain . . . should become an integral part of a European Federation' (quoted in Young, 1985, p. 929). As for a European Army, which he had done so much to inspire, this was now rejected as a 'bucket of wood pulp' (quoted in Carlton, 1986, p. 312).

Considering this kind of sniping which he had to face from Churchill and that of another kind from the 'pro-Europeans', as well as the pressure from the Americans and prospective members of the Defence Community that if Britain felt unable actually to join the EDC she should make commitments to the Community which would effectively imply membership, Eden's position on the EDC remained remarkably consistent. From late 1951 through to the eventual collapse of the project with the failure of the French National Assembly to ratify a laboriously obtained EDC Treaty in August 1954, he maintained that Britain's world position and determination to preserve her sovereignty intact precluded joining the Defence Community. Though his preference was for a non-supranational defence system which would include Germany, no obvious route towards this goal emerged and he had no desire to see Britain castigated as the saboteur of the EDC by putting such an alternative forward. Instead, he did his utmost to ensure that the EDC, but without British membership, should succeed.

This was not entirely a forlorn hope but involved a considerable effort. Although the EDC proposal had originated with the French and although, since February 1951, discussions had been taking place between France, Italy, the Benelux powers and West Germany to set up a European Army, it was France who now demonstrated the most nervousness in proceeding. After opinion in the French Assembly turned markedly against the EDC in the middle of the year, the only way Schuman could hope to secure approval to sign an EDC treaty was by obtaining additional guarantees from Britain which would reduce French fears of Germany being able to attain a dominating influence. Eden's response was a series of concessions to the French (and to the Dutch and Belgians, who by this time had reservations of their own) culminating in the offer of an Anglo-EDC treaty guaranteeing the Defence Community against internal and external threats. Without Eden's conciliatory gestures – and American threats to reduce their financial commitment to NATO — it is difficult to believe that the EDC treaty would ever have been signed at all (Young, 1988a, pp. 83–7).

These were not the actions of a man who, it is sometimes said, wished the EDC to fail. On the contrary, apart from the desire to solve the problem of German rearmament, the EDC was seen as a valuable way of restoring the image of Britain's benevolence towards European unity and counteracting the impression given by the Rome speech. Both objectives no doubt appeared more realizable now that, as the EDC debates proceeded, the federalist elements of the Pleven Plan were edged aside by the more urgent issues of defence. It is true that in the midst of the struggle to have the EDC treaty signed, in January 1952, Eden was unable to refrain from his blunt statement at Columbia University that joining a European federation was 'something we know, in our bones, we cannot do'. But, while this was uncharacteristically undiplomatic of Eden, it was no more than an obvious corollary to his policies. Again it was the tone which made it appear more controversial than it was. Inevitably, such public statements reinforced the view of a negative approach to Europe. The more positive work behind the scenes went unnoticed.

Claims that 'concessions were ... dragged from the reluctant Eden' do the Foreign Secretary an injustice (Carlton, 1986, p. 313). We may be sure that Eden took very seriously Acheson's threats that America would wash her hands of Europe's defence if the Germans were not participants, yet recent research suggests that he was often ahead of the Americans with proposals for compromise. It may be, indeed, that the Columbia speech was a marker to his American hosts of the limits to which British concessions could be allowed to go. In fact, something like a partnership existed between London and Washington on the EDC issue based on a common recognition that Britain had given way as much as she could and that the real obstacle lay in Paris. Eventually, and without conceding on fundamentals — no British membership, but no sabotage — he was given the satisfaction of seeing the EDC treaty signed by the Six in May 1952 (Young, 1988a, pp. 84, 87–8).

This had now to be ratified by the parliaments of the member states. Eden expected it to take a matter of weeks. In fact the process dragged on for two more years, reaching the frustrating conclusion of being rejected by the French Assembly. Meanwhile the French demanded further concessions. Eden, fearful that they might never ratify and with no acceptable alternative to German rearmament other than the EDC, went to extraordinary lengths to satisfy France. In February 1953 he agreed that Britain might be represented in EDC institutions, though not become a full member, and that Britain would undertake to negotiate with the EDC and NATO before British troop levels in Europe were reduced. A year later, this was hiked up to a promise to insert one British division in an EDC corps and to preserve 'the present fighting capacity' of British troops on the Continent (Young, 1988a, pp. 90–1).

It was to no avail. French apprehensions which had existed even at the inception of the Pleven Plan were to be magnified over the following four years. Fears about reviving German militarism, worries about antagonizing the Russians, and concerns about a loss of French identity all meant that there was never a clear majority in support of the EDC in the French Assembly. Escalating difficulties in Indo-China added to French paranoia for, with a large proportion of France's armed forces tied up in Asia, the Germans would contribute more divisions than France to the European Army (Dockrill, 1989, p. 154). Nor were American tactics helpful. The infamous statement by John Foster Dulles, who became Secretary of State in 1953, that unless the French ratified the EDC treaty the United States might have to make an 'agonizing reappraisal' of its defence relations with Europe was just part of a catalogue of such warnings from Dulles and his predecessor. Even if these threats were taken at face value, their effect was to reinforce a growing view in France that the EDC was no longer a European initiative for unity but rather part of a United States strategy for the Americanization of the Continent (Loth, 1988, p. 285).

Though logic suggested it was always the most likely outcome, French rejection of the EDC on 30 August 1954 nevertheless threw the Western Alliance into crisis. Given that France was the author of the project and that most of her prospective partners in a European Army would have preferred a 'NATO solution' to the question of German rearmament, the irritation which now ensued is not surprising. Yet if the 'NATO solution' was all that remained, to press it now might drive France from the North Atlantic Pact. On the other hand, the Americans were again warning of 'reappraisal', i.e. withdrawal from Europe, unless Germany was rearmed. As for the West Germans, who had ratified the EDC treaty in May 1953 following parliamentary debates almost as heated as those in France (the Benelux countries also ratified; the Italians waited to see what the French would do), it appeared a galling full stop to their attempts to achieve the end of military occupation of their country and, thereby, full recognition of their sovereignty.

It was Eden who rescued the situation and prevented the possible collapse of NATO itself. Though he was later to claim that the answer came to him while soaking in his bath, an alternative had, in fact, been gestating for some time and there are at least four claimants to its authorship other than the Foreign Secretary (Charlton, 1983, p. 163; Dockrill, 1989, p. 160; Fursdon, 1980, p. 311; Lamb, 1987, p. 67). The ploy was to use the Brussels Treaty of 1948, rather than NATO, as the platform for bringing German contingents into the defence of Europe. The advantages of the Brussels Pact, over and above the crucial fact that there was no hint of supranationalism in it, were that it allowed for tighter controls over the forces of participating states and that it did not, as did NATO, assume an equality of contribution among its members. If Germany was to be brought into an expanded Brussels Treaty she might then, at a later date, be allowed into NATO fully controlled by the machinery of the Brussels Pact. This was what was to happen, and by the end of May 1955 Germany (and Italy) had joined both the Brussels Treaty – now renamed Western European Union (WEU) – and NATO.

If Eden cannot be allowed full credit for thinking up this solution, the glory of getting it to stick was all his. In a flurry of what now would be called 'shuttle diplomacy', in September 1954 he flew to Brussels, Bonn, Rome and Paris in order to get the new proposal accepted. Dulles, who would have preferred a more supranational package, was forced to comply as he could provide no workable alternative to what Eden had on offer. To cap it all, and to reassure the French, Eden now made a 'revolutionary pledge' to maintain British forces in Europe for as long as the Brussels Treaty Powers wished (Northedge, 1974, p. 169). This was the kind of traditional diplomacy that Eden was best at, and Eisenhower, the American President, praised the outcome as one of the 'greatest diplomatic achievements of our time' (quoted in Bartlett, 1977, p. 109). Spaak later asserted that 'Eden saved the Atlantic alliance' (quoted in Young, 1988a, p. 101). Praise indeed from a 'European' who had been so dismayed by Eden's Rome speech in 1951.

Had Eden intended the collapse of the EDC all along? Had he 'secretly recognized that such an outcome might open the way to a solution more congenial to him' (Carlton, 1986, p. 361)? We know that, as early as 1951, he had considered an alternative similar to that which would emerge four years later as WEU. Yet preparing for eventual failure is not the same as wishing that failure to happen. Still less did it involve working towards it. All the evidence suggests that Eden, rather unimaginatively perhaps, was prepared to work with what he had inherited. After all, he firmly desired German rearmament – largely because the Americans did – and, so long as Britain was not caught up in any of its federalist aspects, the EDC seemed to hold the best chances of bringing this about. His only concession to the European idea – and it was not an inconsiderable one in the circumstances – was that he would do nothing which might bring about its collapse. This was a far from negative stance and Eden made rather more concessions than were appropriate for a government intent merely on keeping its hands clean. When, in the midst of the ratification struggle, he was urged by Macmillan and others to put an end to appeasing the French and instead prepare an alternative to the EDC, he refused to listen. If, even so, his actions sometimes appeared grudging this was born of a concern not to be drawn by degrees into actual membership of the EDC and of a recognition of the danger that whatever the French were offered, they would soon demand more (Young, 1988a, pp. 90, 92, 101–2). However, because this more positive approach via concessions attracted little publicity, the seemingly dismissive tone of the Rome and Columbia speeches was not eradicated.

In the promise not to withdraw from Europe without the agreement of WEU, Eden, it has been argued, 'was now urging a course which he had persistently and scornfully rejected and might have saved the EDC had it been made earlier' (Shlaim, Jones and Sainsbury, 1977, p. 101). This is a variant on the thesis, publicly stated by the French politician Paul Reynaud in 1951, that Britain's refusal to participate in a European Army was bound to lead to the demise of the EDC (Fursdon, 1980, p. 129). Neither view fits the facts. In the first place, Eden had already offered commitments not very different to those associated with WEU before the EDC had collapsed. (Dockrill, 1989, p. 153; Northedge, 1974, pp. 163, 168). They had had little impact. Perhaps it was the case that 'the French Assembly had a deep, psychological need to reject at least once a European settlement involving the Germans' (Carlton, 1986, p. 363). It is arguable that Eden, having gone so far in reducing Britain's freedom of action under WEU, might have gone the whole hog and gained further political kudos by joining the EDC. But such a step was far from necessary, as in reality little had, even now, been given away. 'It can be cancelled at any time ...,' Churchill asserted of the British promise. 'It does not mean anything. All words ... Never ... was the leadership of Europe so cheaply won' (quoted in Carlton, 1986, p. 363). And this was not just Churchillian rhetoric. Within three years Britain was seeking the reduction of her continental forces on the ground of 'too heavy a strain on the external finances of the UK', as the WEU agreement allowed. Ultimately, it was the psychological impact of the British offer rather than any essential change in British policy which was important (Bartlett, 1977, p. 109; Dockrill, 1989, pp. 162, 166–7; Northedge, 1974, p. 169).

It seems highly unlikely, in any case, that an earlier or more comprehensive British commitment to the EDC would have made much difference to the final outcome. Divisions of opinion in France were so stark that it would have taken more than this to have papered over them. On top of this, fears amongst the Dutch, Belgians and Italians that France was out to dominate the EDC grew in proportion to the increased French demands on Britain. The Germans, nursing their own profound apprehensions about the Defence Community, were increasingly reluctant to follow the French down a path which seemed to depart from the model desired by the Americans (Loth, 1988, p. 284).

Though Eden's attitude probably contributed materially, if not decisively, to the death of the EDC he acted as he did – loath to be the cause of failure, producing an alternative once failure had occurred – precisely because he wished to avoid adding to Britain's reputation as a reluctant supporter of European cooperation. His stance was largely vindicated by the disarray in which the federalists now found themselves over the EDC. An initiative from the Six to set up a European Political Community (EPC) which would provide the necessary organic links between the EDC and the ECSC had withered away by mid-1954 (Loth, 1988, p. 286; Willis, 1968, pp. 158–61). In truth, the project had been misconceived from the start, having been only imperfectly thought through and with its fundamental objective, the containment of a re-armed Germany, hamstrung by an overzealous injection of federalism including the unrealistic expectation that the British, who had rejected supranational control over their industries, would swallow abdication of sovereignty over their armed forces. It was a case, as the French Premier, Mendes-France, said in another connection, of 'too much supranationality too suddenly' (quoted in Dockrill, 1989, p. 162).

Conversely, Eden's creation, WEU, now seemed to offer the best hope of developing a wider form of European cooperation. It had its

56

own Council and Parliamentary Assembly made up of Britain together with the Six. Moreover, the treaty which provided its legal basis declared that it was the intention of these states to 'promote the unity and to encourage the progressive integration of Europe' (quoted in Camps, 1964, p. 18). In other words, WEU appeared a triumph for Britain's preference for loose, inter-governmental cooperation and added, temporarily at least, to Britain's credibility in Europe. By contrast, the federalist position had received a, largely self-inflicted, setback. The ECSC, in operation since early 1953, could easily be viewed as the high-water mark of the Western Europeans' commitment to supra-nationality, and even this seemed endangered after the EDC fiasco. 'One cannot hide the fact', a contemporary commentator noted, 'that the annoying adventure of the Defence Community Treaty, which [Monnet] championed, has dealt ECSC a very heavy blow from which it will have difficulty in recovering' (quoted in Willis, 1968, p. 226). In the winter of 1954, Monnet announced his intention to step down as President of the High Authority of the ECSC.

The whole trend of British policy towards the, now seemingly ephemeral, European movement, providing encouragement from without but keeping a cautious distance, could be reasonably assumed to have been vindicated. And, if we return to the early months of the Conservative Government, we can see that WEU was merely the most successful of a series of attempts to provide a loose association between Britain and more formal continental developments. The first of these had been the so called 'Eden Plan' which sought, during 1952, to mesh the organs of the existing Council of Europe with those of the emerging ECSC and EDC. Monnet read British intentions as disruptive. This was unfair, though Monnet continued to be suspicious and to use his influence as President of the High Authority of the ECSC to fend off the British.

Undismayed, the British examined alternative means of association in the form of an Anglo-ECSC treaty. At first the approach was characteristically cautious. Monnet's suggestions of close procedural links between Britain and the ECSC were rebuffed on the grounds that the Coal and Steel Community had not yet shown that it could work and might yet be brought to nothing by the controversy over the EDC. There was clearly some room for these doubts. The climate changed a little early in 1953 when Schuman was replaced as French Foreign Minister by the non-federalist Bidault. Moreover, the supra-nationalism which had played such a significant part in the early

57

debates on the Schuman Plan had had to be modified in the final ECSC agreement in order to placate the Benelux countries who feared overweening influence in the Community by their larger partners. The resulting High Authority was not sovereign but answerable to a special Council of Ministers whose members existed to protect the national interest of their own state. This shortfall from the earlier Monnet–Schuman ideals gave some comfort to the British in that their own preference for inter-governmental cooperation seemed to be in the ascendancy and supranationalism in decline. But the lessons to be learned were double-edged. Britain could either wait and watch this apparent dissolution from a distance, or she might act more positively, gaining kudos and political advantage from her actions.

To its credit, the Foreign Office decided to pursue the latter course and in January 1954 Eden went so far as to recommend to the Cabinet that Britain pursue a limited, i.e. non-supranational, common market in steel with the ECSC. The thinking behind this was essentially twofold. First, there was the highly significant recognition that the ECSC was likely to be an economic entity of importance and that Britain could not afford to ignore it. British steel, being more competitive than coal, could pioneer the economic association which it was accepted should develop between the two. There was also the hope that a Treaty of Association along these lines would boost the supporters of the EDC. But the scheme met resistance from representatives of the British steel industry, who seemed less sanguine about the eventual success of the ECSC than did the Foreign Office, and, reminiscent of Ernest Bevin's earlier difficulties, also from a doubtful Board of Trade. These obstacles, plus the French failure to ratify the EDC treaty, robbed the project of its momentum. An Anglo-ECSC Treaty of Association was actually signed in December 1954 but it was a much more uninspiring affair than the Foreign Office had proposed earlier in the year. Under the terms of the agreement a Council of Association was brought into being which allowed Britain and the ECSC states formal channels of consultation; but considering that a British delegation to the Community had been working in Luxembourg since September 1952 this was hardly a remarkable move forward (Young, 1988b, pp. 124–9).

The Treaty of Association did little to enhance Britain's reputation amongst supporters of integration and has provided kindling to the fires of critics of Eden's lack of vision as Foreign Secretary. Eden, it is argued, 'had great flair but no genius. Unlike Bevin he was a tactician not a strategist, a rifleman setting his sights on "definite but limited problems" eschewing "wide general discussion"' (Adamthwaite, 1988, p. 13). His three pillars of British foreign policy – the United States, the Commonwealth and, trailing last, Europe – were 'very much watered-down Winston' (Shlaim, 1978, p. 91). Innovation towards Europe, it is implied, was hardly to be expected of someone who dismissed Churchill's European Union Movement as 'a party stunt', who claimed to be 'an Atlantic animal' and who condemned criticism of Britain's stance on the EDC in the Council of Europe with the words, 'Strasbourg was always a misfortune; it is now nearly a calamity' (quoted in Shlaim, 1978, p. 99; Lamb, 1987, p. 62).

Yet Eden's actions as Churchill's Foreign Secretary from 1951 to 1955 were far more 'pro-European' than this would suggest. While Europe did not hold a high priority for him and his daily agenda was often made up of concerns which he judged more pressing, Eden was quite prepared to see the cause of supranationalism advance in Western Europe so long as Britain was not expected to become actively involved (Charlton, 1983, p. 152). All, however, was by no means governed by *laissez-faire*. The 'Eden Plan' of 1952 was a positive attempt to breathe new life into the Council of Europe and live up to Britain's promise to associate herself with the Schuman Plan. Eden intended the actual Treaty of Association of December 1954 to include the radical departure of an Anglo-ECSC common market in steel, but this foundered under opposition from British industry and the Board of Trade.

This brings us back to the EDC. Though Eden's motives here were primarily governed by considerations of defence rather than integration, in most minds federalism came to be obscured by these same considerations as the debate on a European Army lengthened. And if Britain's attitude towards Europe was on trial over the EDC it was also increasingly viewed as a test of the momentum of federalism. Put in simple terms, at the start of 1955 it looked distinctly as though Eden had won and the federalists had lost. Britain and the Six, within the non-supranational WEU, appeared a better bet for the future of European cooperation than did the Six alone driving down the apparent dead-end towards supranationality.

This understandable, if erroneous, conclusion was reinforced when hard facts were taken into account. Britain's GNP remained twice that of the West Germans and almost three times that of France. She was still, after the United States, the second most significant power in the Western world. Trade with the Commonwealth made up 49 per cent of her imports, 54 per cent of her exports and 65 per cent of her external investments. Such figures might explain why even the thoughts of a so-called 'pro-European' like Macmillan turned, as had Bevin's before him, to the idea of creating an economic bloc out of the Empire which might rival those of the Superpowers (Charlton, 1983, p. 130). In fact, the 'pro-Europeans' in the Conservative Party, such as Macmillan, Maxwell-Fyfe and Duncan Sandys, never produced anything other than variants on Eden's European schemes and certainly nothing which so submerged the British antipathy to supranationalism that it might be acceptable to Monnet and his colleagues. Yet this ground was already shifting. British trade with the Commonwealth had reached its apogee and began to fall. Economic power began to shift perceptibly in the favour of the Western Europeans. Equally significantly, the European federalists soon demonstrated their resilience by instigating revival of the European Idea – *'La Relance Européenne'*. Again they were to make a significant advance and, once more, the British were to be left behind.

6

On the Sidelines, 1955—58

1955 was a crucial year. *La Relance*, the re-launch of the integration-ist idea, led to the conference of the Six at Messina, Sicily which, in turn, produced the European Economic Community. Standing at the crossroads, the British misread the signs and spent almost twenty years down what turned out to be one of the great side-tracks of post-war history. Yet it was not clear, even to themselves, what the Six at Messina wanted, whether all could agree to the customs union which was the eventual outcome or whether an alterna-tive British proposal of a more modest free trade grouping would not find more general acceptance. The British, it follows from this, were somewhat less obstinately wrong-headed than is sometimes implied. Historians have tended to take their cue from often guilty confessions of British participants in these events and to write in terms of 'costly failure' and of 'passing up (the) invitation ... to join the Europeans' (Shlaim, 1978, p. 102; Charlton, 1983, p. 196). Though the danger of being un-historical lurks in this, the trend continues in more recent studies (Lamb, 1987, p. 101; Sanders, 1990, p. 138). Attempts made in earlier analyses to deal more sympathetically with the British dilemma (Camps, 1964; Northedge, 1974) seem to be supported by work based on a scholarly examination of recently opened archives (Young, 1989).

Impetus for the 're-launch' did not spring from any clear evidence that the ECSC had been successful. Though there were indications that the experiment was working, the picture in 1955 remained a mixed one in terms of economic performance and the willingness of the member states to bow to the edicts of the High Authority. The most concrete signs of progress came in the years immediately *after* the 're-launch' (Willis, 1968, pp. 228–34). As ever, pragmatism was the spur. To many Europeans, further integration appeared the only practical way of maintaining the impetus of post-war economic reconstruction amongst the nation states. This was especially the case with the smaller powers such as the Dutch who were fearful that without developments towards a common market their position as exporters of agricultural produce would be eroded (Milward, 1987, p. 442). Significantly, it was the Dutch Foreign Minister, Johan Beyen, who, in the spring of 1955, suggested a conference of the Six which he intended should initiate a general customs union as the next stage in European integration. Although Beyen's suggestion was eagerly received by Monnet and by Spaak, both favoured the ECSC model of a long-term, rolling process of integration, economic sector by economic sector, rather than a leap into an all-embracing customs union. This difference of opinion over strategy was not resolved at the conference of the Six which was held at Messina in June.

These sorts of division played a significant part in nourishing British scepticism about what the Six hoped to achieve. It was, after all, less than a year after the collapse of the EDC project and, seemingly, the hopes of the federalists too. The very terminology, 're-launch', clearly suggests an attempt to regain lost momentum. There were other obvious signs too of a division of interests amongst the participants at Messina. The French, though willing to contemplate the extension of the existing Community to cover other areas of cooperation, were now firmly against raising the troublesome issue of supranationalism. A priority for them at Messina was to develop European cooperation in the peaceful uses of atomic energy, which was an area too costly to embark upon alone. Monnet too was keen that atomic energy be the next sector to be integrated by the Six. With interesting caution, however, the French Government resisted Monnet's attempts to stay on as President of the ECSC now that a re-launch seemed a possibility, and backed a less avidly 'European' candidate (Camps, 1964, pp. 22–9). The Germans did not send a high-ranking Minister to Messina. This reflected a fissure between the federalist views of Adenauer and those of his Finance Minister, Ludwig Erhard, who preferred an inter-governmental approach to cooperation through an organization such as the OEEC – a split which was to give groundless comfort to the British for some time.

The disdain of later commentators that Britain did not even send a representative to Messina is misplaced (Charlton, 1983, p. 169; Lamb,

1987, p. 68). She was not invited to do so. This does not seem to imply any deliberate intention on the part of the Six to isolate the British. Britain was given advance information of Beyen's proposals and a resolution at the Messina conference implied that the United Kingdom would be brought into discussions on the next steps forward – though the formal invitation to this effect was rather slow in coming. The British were content with this, for nothing occurred at Messina to perturb them. The need to cater for the mixed motives of the governments represented there meant that the tone of the final communiqué was more cautious than intended by those most closely associated with the re-launch. Though a determination to set up 'a European Common Market, free from all tariffs and quantitative restrictions' was the declared objective, no indication as to how this might be done, whether via a customs union or a free trade area, or how long the process might take, was provided. Moreover, references to supranationalism were glaringly absent. It is not surprising, therefore, that British officials should have felt that the Europeans were edging towards the British 'intergovernmental method', that practicalities had not been thought through and that 'no very spectacular developments are to be expected as a result of the Messina conference' (quoted in Young, 1989, p. 201).

Thus far, British actions ran entirely true to form. Their preference, if they had to choose, was for the free trade route forward rather than a customs union. This tied in more with a rather uncoordinated movement towards trade liberalization through reductions in European tariffs and quotas which was being generally conducted via the OEEC. A customs union, conversely, implied a more rigid common external tariff which was bound to have a radical effect on existing British trade patterns, particularly with the preferential system developed within the Commonwealth. Fundamental to this was the cheap food which Britain was able to obtain from the Commonwealth. This would be certain to be put at risk by a customs union and although agriculture was not discussed at Messina, 'it was axiomatic that if a common market was to be produced an agreement on what to do about agriculture would have to be reached' (Milward, 1987, p. 460). The British were also wary that a customs union might, willy-nilly, be a slide towards supranationalism. These considerations ruled it out. On the other hand, they would not be saboteurs and were prepared to pursue the possibility of an association along the lines they had with the ECSC. Meanwhile, they agreed to have representation on the inter-governmental committee, chaired by the pro-European

Belgian statesman Paul-Henri Spaak, which was to meet in Brussels in order to carry the Messina resolution forward. Though, mainly because of the EDC episode, there was little expectation that these discussions would come to much, a British presence would allow them to deflect criticisms of being 'anti-European', to consolidate the desired integration of Germany into Western Europe and, a most harmful misjudgement, permit the negotiations to be influenced in a direction more acceptable to London.

The nature of British representation on this Spaak Committee has come under a great deal of criticism. Wrangles in Whitehall over whether the British member of the committee should be a delegate, as the Foreign Office wished, or merely an 'observer', as the Treasury preferred, is a revealing insight into the continuing desire on the part of the economic departments to distance themselves from developments in Europe. The Foreign Office, hoped to build on the prestige earned by the achievement of WEU and guide the Europeans along acceptable lines. The compromise term of 'representative' may be judged a marginal victory for the Foreign Office view. On the other hand, this 'representative' was a civil servant from the Board of Trade, a clear, probably deliberate rather than merely clumsy, signal that Britain considered the discussions to be essentially economic and not political. A myth has developed that this Board of Trade official at the Brussels talks, Russell Bretherton, adopted a smug and aloof stance, though it seems beyond doubt that Bretherton efficiently and cooperatively presented his Government's point of view (Charlton, 1983, p. 181; Young, 1989, p. 205). The problem rather was that the Foreign Office's position was flawed. The close collaboration they desired at Brussels as a means of diverting the Europeans was fine, so long as it worked. If the reverse occurred, the British could find themselves entangled in decisions which were unpalatable to them. This, in effect, was what happened. And, as Young points out,

> These dangers ought really to have been obvious from the start, especially after London's experience with the Schuman Plan in 1950; one reason for avoiding the Schuman Plan talks had been the fear of becoming embroiled by implication, or being forced into an embarrassing withdrawal if the talks did not move Britain's way. At that time the Conservatives had pressed the Government to enter the talks under reservations. Now they were seeing what problems such a course could have created. (Young, 1989, p. 206)

This judgement seems a little harsh, for the outcome of Messina seemed to indicate that the divisions amongst the Six between those who wanted a customs union and those who might settle for a free trade area left plenty of room for British influence to come into play. As late as October, Bretherton felt able to report that there was 'little emphasis on supranational authority' in the Spaak Committee and it also seemed unlikely that France or the Germans would go along with a common market (Lamb, 1987, p. 73; Young, 1989, p. 207). These turned out to be pipe-dreams. Young suggests that although Spaak had played down supranationalism his intention from the beginning was to move discussions down that path. In this sense, the British had been brought into the talks under false pretences (Young, 1989, p. 217). Spaak referred at the time to the necessity for 'a more diplomatic', a 'more Machiavellian', a 'more subtle' approach to supranationalism than had existed during the ECSC and EDC debates (quoted in Camps, 1964, p. 41). If this was his strategy he was doing no more than to influence the proceedings in a manner, though not a direction, similar to the British. It seems hardly likely, however, that even the dynamic chairmanship of Spaak could alone have caused the shift at Brussels away from the sector approach to a general acceptance of a common market. He was aided by two coincidental and unpredictable events: signs of a reassertion in the German government of the dominance of Adenauer's ideas over those, like Erhard, who were more reluctant integrationists, and a more positive approach on the part of the French (Camps, 1964, pp. 32–3). Even so, the British may have over-reacted to these shifts and misread their significance, for the final resolutions of the Spaak Committee at the end of 1955 continued to be 'cautious and circumspect' over the question of supranationality (Camps, 1964, p. 49).

By the end of September there was already, however, a strong movement in London to disengage from the Brussels talks. This was inspired principally by the Treasury, where arguments about the damage a common market would wreak with the Commonwealth and British industry continued to be pressed. The Foreign Office dithered and the break did not come until 7 November, when Bretherton was withdrawn from the Brussels negotiations for fear of being drawn into unacceptable decisions. Before this, however, Spaak, who by now had a clear picture of British reservations and was prompted from the wings by Monnet, had already cut the Gordian knot and excluded them from any contribution to the final report of the Committee (Young, 1989, p. 209). Withdrawal was bad enough and left the

British in worse odour than if, as at Messina, no representative had been present at all. What was worse was the deceit and ineptitude which now coloured British policy, allowing them for the first time justifiably to be accused of attempting to wreck the plans for European integration which were now emerging.

Since Messina, the British had frequently stated their preference for advances in European economic cooperation to take place within the inter-governmental framework of the OEEC. There had always been something disingenuous about this. Lamb points out that the OEEC had declined in importance by 1955 and that the British had had a hand in this process by initiating cuts in the OEEC budget (p. 70). This view is given some support by Young who notes that, after Messina, Macmillan, by this time Foreign Secretary, admitted that the OEEC was in decline and that the Council of Europe might become the focus of European cooperation (Young, 1989, p. 220). The British none the less had continued to press the OEEC as an alternative route for further cooperation in the Spaak Committee. This was initially accepted by the Six as a legitimate negotiating position, though the intransigence of the British soon became an increasing source of annoyance and by the time they had withdrawn from the Spaak Committee in November it was seen for what it was, a delaying tactic (Camps, 1964, p. 40).

But the British went further than this. They now decided to approach the Germans and inform them that Britain rejected the idea of a common market. The intention was to play off the Erhard faction against the 'federalists' surrounding Adenauer in the hope of reasserting German resistance to a customs union. 'If we were to give them a lead', the Cabinet supposed, 'the Germans might decide not to join a common market and to concentrate on cooperation through OEEC' (quoted in Lamb, 1987, p. 77). Simultaneously, the British decided to play on anticipated American fears of a threat to a liberal economic system. The British Government was opposed to a common market, Washington was told, not out of any selfish concerns about the Commonwealth, but out of apprehension over the creation of a discriminatory economic bloc in the heart of Europe. While this was going on, in November, R. A. Butler, the Chancellor of the Exchequer, met first Beyen and then Spaak in London, leading them both to believe not just that Britain would be happy to form an association with a common market if it emerged, but, quite falsely, that the British might even join it (Charlton, 1983, p. 190; Lamb, 1987, pp. 75–8). A policy of 'asserting influence' had been transformed, almost imperceptibly, into one of 'sabotage'.

It backfired calamitously. The British were consistently to overestimate their bargaining power at this juncture and this was a striking example. Adenauer was more fully in command of European policy in the German Government than was realized in London. His hand was strengthened by a coincidental downturn in East–West relations which reaffirmed the Eisenhower Administration's desire for a strong, integrated Europe with West Germany playing a full part. Again, it is possible to detect Monnet at work, using his influence with the Americans to counter any British leverage. Neither Bonn nor Washington was ready to listen to the British. At the same time, now that the Germans had been told of British rejection of a common market, London was forced publicly to come clean. Possibly this was the reason for the action which the British government now took (Young, 1989, p. 214). A less sympathetic view is that the main intention was still to destroy the schemes of the Europeans (Lamb, 1987, pp. 80–1). Given the circumstances of the British announcement that they would not join the Six, it is difficult not to accept the latter interpretation. This was made at a meeting of the OEEC Council rather than to the ECSC. Moreover, it came on 7 December, just before the publication of the final report of the Spaak Committee. Both Beyen and Spaak read it as sabotage and felt especially betrayed by Butler. The effects were possibly long-lasting and it may well be that from the resentment generated 'stemmed the Messina powers' refusal to associate Britain with the Common Market through a Free Trade Area when Macmillan was Prime Minister in 1957 and 1958' (Lamb, 1987, p. 79).

But this was no isolated occurrence and British actions remained a continual source of dismay to the Europeans. The view that 'the period of British hostility to the plans of the Six was short-lived' is not easy to sustain in the light of recent research (Camps, 1964, p. 92). The Spaak Report, recommending the creation of a customs union and a European Atomic Authority (Euratom), was eventually produced at the beginning of 1956. It was accepted by the Foreign Ministers of the Six at a meeting in Venice in May. The negotiators at Brussels were now given the task of producing a formal treaty based on this agreement. Following this, the two treaties setting up the EEC and Euratom were signed in Rome in March 1957. By January 1958 they had been ratified by the governments of the participating states and the European Economic Community came into operation – less than three years after the re-launch had been initiated. In the meantime, as this progression took place, the view in the Foreign Office was that 'we have to see if we can discourage the

67

Six from going ahead without risking incurring their displeasure by coming out in open opposition to their ideals' and Macmillan, Chancellor of the Exchequer since December 1955, asked his Treasury officials to produce an alternative to the Messina proposals which could act as 'a rearguard action or an advance' (quoted in Lamb, 1987, pp. 87–8).

The assumption in Whitehall after publication of the Spaak Report was that there was plenty of time to draw up a rival scheme, as agreement among the Six on how to proceed on its recommendations was unlikely. This was not an unrealistic view and the astonishing speed of the Europeans was no doubt a surprise to the Six themselves. The French, for instance, were much more interested in Euratom than in the customs union and there were concerns, especially amongst the Benelux powers, that Paris might accept the former but not the latter. Monnet himself shared the French emphasis and, because 'atoms were news and could be dramatized in a way that quotas and tariffs could not,' viewed this as the best way of recharging the momentum for the building of Europe (Camps, 1964, p. 55). Spaak did not take this view. In this he was aligned with the Germans, who were lukewarm, even antipathetic towards Euratom. These differences, plus the even more intricate questions of where agriculture would fit into the common market and how, as France had insisted at the Venice meeting, French overseas territories could be associated with the project, had to be settled. In these circumstances, the British were able to delude themselves that Spaak would 'no doubt fall over himself' to support a scheme of their own for a Free Trade Area made up of OEEC countries which would then associate itself with the Six (Lamb, 1987, p. 93).

To a significant degree, this Free Trade Area (FTA) proposition, or Plan G as the British called it, was a spoiling tactic aimed at winning over those amongst the Messina group who were half-hearted about a customs union. It was, as the Cabinet admitted in June 1956, a 'diversion' and the underlying hope was that the recommendations of the Spaak Report would be stillborn (Lamb, 1987, p. 95). But this underestimated the underlying determination of the Six to follow through the Messina declaration to the end and a readiness, especially on the part of the Germans, to make quite significant concessions to achieve this.

As the realization that this was indeed the case began to dawn early in 1956, Plan G started to take on the shape of a more distinct alternative to the Spaak proposals, rather than just a wrecking procedure. Economically, its attraction was that while the common market intended to work by stages towards a single external tariff, a free trade system would simply regulate the internal tariffs and quotas of its members, leaving each of them free to set its own duties on external trade from outside the group. This would leave Commonwealth Preferences untouched; the more so as it would be concerned, upon the insistence of the British — and against the wishes of their OEEC partners — entirely with industrial, not agricultural, products. Politically, the Free Trade Area would not impinge upon national sovereignty. The EEC and Euratom, in contrast, were both imbued with the supranational ideal, if in more subdued tones than had been the case with the ECSC and the EDC.

But officials had now become increasingly fearful that if Europe really did begin to organize itself, Britain could not afford to stay out. The spectre beckoned of a loss of British leadership on the Continent and of her position as a bridge between the United States and the Europeans. The prospect also had to be faced that a customs union of the Six would, by definition, be discriminatory towards British trade. A Free Trade Area linked to the Six would eliminate this danger. This, in itself, was enough to produce a sizeable shift in British thinking — though not a big enough reassessment to allow them to contemplate joining the Six. A statement by Macmillan to the Cabinet in September 1956 that 'our economy could not be sustained indefinitely on the basis of a protected and well insulated market' was a signal that Plan G might be a halting step away from a quarter of a century of British protectionism and towards a low-tariff area within Europe (quoted in Lamb, 1987, p. 97). It may be that the British expected the Six to acknowledge this significant reorientation of policy as in itself a signal of good intent by any waverers in the Messina group; though in reality what was on offer was not much more than a more sophisticated version of a form of 'association' put forward since the announcement of the Schuman Plan.

'Association', whether with the ECSC or the EDC, had always held the implication that Britain would obtain advantages without significantly adding to her obligations. This was more than ever the case with the notion of developing an FTA and associating it with the Six. The overwhelming advantages for Britain were patent. She would be able to export her industrial manufactures to the Continent in breach of the common tariff to be erected by the Six, and to continue to receive cheap food and raw materials from the Commonwealth. Not surprisingly the Europeans were inclined to question the propriety

69

of this. In addition, Britain's conversion to the abandonment of protection was neither perfectly complete nor entirely genuine and the desire simply to ruin the customs union was never far from the surface. In 1957, even as the EEC was crystallizing, Macmillan warned his colleagues,

> We must not be bullied ... We could if we were driven to it, fight their movement ... We must take positive action in this field, to ensure that the wider Free Trade Area is more attractive than the narrower Common Market of the Six. We must take the lead either in widening their project or, if they will not cooperate with us, in opposing it. (quoted in Mowat, 1973, p. 148)

The Six were not blind to all this; and British assertions that they did not wish to upset the plan for a customs union failed to eliminate suspicions that the FTA was 'a clever move to induce France to stop short of the full integration process' or 'simply a mischievous move to torpedo the Continental efforts by raising false hopes of an even larger plan' (Camps, 1964, pp. 101, 108). The surprise is really that Britain's Plan G held so much mileage. It was not finally abandoned until the end of 1958; and not before, some would argue, it had come within reach of success. Uncertainties amongst various political and economic sections in both Germany and France over the benefits to be earned from a customs union, highlighted during the debates in national parliaments before the ratification of the Treaty of Rome during the summer of 1957, played a significant part in making the looser British proposal appear attractive (Willis, 1968, pp. 251–72). At one stage, to the dismay of Spaak and the elation of the British, it looked as though French demands for preferential terms for her colonies, her agriculture and her social policies would wreck the customs union negotiations. Fearful of a repetition of the EDC fiasco and concerned to reach agreement before less 'European-minded' governments emerged in France and Germany, Spaak and Adenauer acceded to the French demands. This, in turn, worried the Dutch who felt that too much had been given away. The Benelux countries, in any case, favoured an arrangement with the British as a counterweight to the influence of their larger neighbours.

But such supposed advantages to the British position could not hide the reality, even amongst those inclined to be sympathetic, that any association of an OEEC Free Trade Area with the Six's common market would require such extraordinary administrative juggling as to

70

be virtually impractical. This may have fed the suspicions of those who felt that the British were, in any case, not serious. As a sign of their good faith, in August 1957 the British set up a committee, chaired by a Minister, Reginald Maudling, rather than a civil servant, to thrash out the case for the FTA link with those who had now signed the Treaty of Rome. At the same time, Britain demonstrated some willingness to meet the concerns of her prospective partners over future tariff policy (Northedge, 1974, pp. 334–5). One authority argues that if these conciliatory moves had been made earlier the policy of association 'would almost have succeeded' (Camps, 1964, p. 169). This is, of course, an imponderable, though it perhaps fails to take into account the resentment amongst some Europeans that the British were trying to have the best of both worlds or the feeling, which refused to evaporate, that they were not out to extend integration but to scotch it. Both added fuel to the arguments of the 'Europeans' that, one way or another, FTA association would simply swamp the common market.

British actions during the spring of 1957 were hardly calculated to ease these apprehensions. In May, Selwyn Lloyd, Foreign Secretary since December 1955, laid out his rather pompously titled 'Grand Design' to rationalize the representative bodies of the various European institutions which had proliferated since the war – Council of Europe, NATO, WEU, ECSC – into a single assembly. Though, like the 'Eden Plan' of early 1952, it tapped a widespread recognition that this was a desirable objective, the attempt to bring 'Atlantic' and 'European', integrationalist and inter-governmental institutions under one roof was taken as evidence of a British refusal to understand the direction in which Europe was now travelling. This was underlined by a British decision, less than three years since the creation of WEU, to reduce its forces on the Continent.

In the end, British ambitions regarding the FTA – whatever they may have amounted to – were destroyed by General de Gaulle in November 1958. De Gaulle had returned as President of France five months earlier to solve the Algerian crisis which had left the nation teetering on the edge of civil war. He was by no means a 'European' in the Monnet mould and the Gaullists had been virulent critics of supranationalism throughout the fifties. But de Gaulle was determined to revive the international status of France and saw the development of a loose European confederation in which national identity would be enhanced rather than submerged – a 'Europe of states' rather than a 'United States of Europe' – as a way of achieving this.

Germany was the chosen partner. Britain, because of her 'Atlanticism' and because of what he considered personal slights suffered at British hands in the recent past, was to be excluded. This process began on 14 November when the French walked out of the Maudling Committee, effectively bringing negotiations on an association with a Free Trade Area to an end. De Gaulle's action was characteristically unilateral. Of the other members of the Six only the Germans may have had some inkling of what he was about to do. Of course, any of the Six might have resisted the French action. They did not. It was the first real test of loyalty to the Treaty of Rome.

With the EEC in being and their plans for association smothered, the logical step now was for the British to form a Free Trade Area with those OEEC states who, like themselves, felt unable to join the Economic Community. This she did and in July 1959 signed the Stockholm Convention, which joined Britain, Austria, Denmark, Norway, Portugal, Sweden and Switzerland together in the European Free Trade Association (EFTA). A free trade area in industrial goods by 1970, not integration, was the objective which the Association set itself. The motives surrounding the setting up of EFTA were predominantly negative ones. This is not surprising given the unpleasant circumstances in which the Maudling Committee broke up. *The Times* condemned 'France the Wrecker' and there was much talk of the French having further divided Europe and of a possible trade war between the Six and those left outside (Camps, 1964, p. 174). Retaliation was a strong inducement for the 'Outer Seven', as significantly they were now being called, to get together. This involved not only a desire for preparedness against a trade war, which did not in fact materialize, but also a strong sense of reprisal, of the need to hit back. This was a sensation which the Seven held in common. For Britain in particular there was the need to organize an alternative to the EEC in order to prevent more states drifting into the ambit of the Six, leaving Britain isolated. The argument is sometimes put that the principal purpose of EFTA was to keep the Seven together so that they might negotiate the better with the Six, presumably by bringing economic pressure to bear (Northedge, 1974, p. 336). This seems unlikely. Pressure of this kind would have been most effective on Paris, yet French trade with the EFTA countries was the lowest of all the members of the EEC. And what would have been the intention of such pressure? To bring the British closer to the EEC? Membership of EFTA was likely to complicate rather than ease such a process. Indeed, joining EFTA was a sign that the British stance on integration had not yet shifted.

But EFTA was a most unsatisfactory alternative for the British – not even a 'second best', as they had, at this point, no clear idea of what was desirable. Because it was not cast in the 'heroic' mould of the 'European' EEC it was difficult to justify it in progressive or idealistic terms. On the more pragmatic level, Britain's partners in the Seven were clearly not industrial giants and it was understood from the outset that low-tariff economies such as Switzerland and Sweden were likely to gain more from a free trade area than was relatively high-tariff Britain. Indeed, between 1960 and 1962 Britain's trade with the EEC increased faster than with EFTA, although technically British exports were discriminated against by the former and favoured by the latter (Camps, 1964, pp. 216–17, 231). Within two years of the signing of the Stockholm Convention it had become clear that Britain was dangerously on the periphery, and she decided to jettison EFTA.

That this period proved to be a turning point can hardly be denied; though whether Britain and her leaders are to be blamed for missing it may be questioned. Looking back over the immediate post-war period, the EEC was, at least partly, the product of a set of economic developments which, by circumstance, Britain was outside, which were not clearly discernible, and over which she had little control. The first three years after the war had seen a generally vigorous expansion of foreign trade throughout Western Europe. Britain had shared in this initial growth but, by the end of the forties, was unable to sustain it. In Western Europe, particularly amongst future founder-members of the EEC, or Little Europe as they are sometimes called, the boom continued. A prominent, though by no means exclusive, reason for this was the differing trading patterns between Britain and her European neighbours. Whereas the Europeans tended to trade with each other, British markets were predominantly outside Europe, with the Commonwealth in particular. What might seem an advantageous position, and one which British leaders strove to maintain, was in reality a handicap. Tied to markets which were more diverse and less vigorous than those developing in post-war Europe, Britain was deprived of the necessary competitive thrust to maintain early post-war growth. The very opposite happened on the Continent where intra-European competition between a group of expanding economies allowed growth to be sustained (Cairncross, 1985, pp. 276–7; Milward, 1987, pp. 335–9). According to Milward, 'Over the period 1948–50 ... British exports stood still ... while Little Europe's exports to Western Europe increased by a half, and by more than a third to the rest of the world' (p. 352).

Here were the roots of those economic arguments which were put forward in the early fifties in support of a regulated, integrated market which Monnet, Schuman and others wanted for sometimes rather different reasons. Such a system, it was argued, would allow European prosperity to continue. In an increasingly economically interdependent region, a policy of tariff reduction, such as the OEEC favoured, was judged both inadequate and potentially divisive. This was most strongly felt amongst the weaker economies of Little Europe, for example the Dutch, for whom the solution to preserving the vitality of their essential agricultural exports lay in a process of European integration. At the same time, the French, who had been early proponents of a customs union so long as it contained Britain, soon changed their view. Because of British economic sluggishness, and because of their susceptibility to American demands and performance, a customs union came to be seen as perfectly possible and even desirable without the British (Milward, 1987, pp. 337, 434). What this suggests, of course, is that opportunities had been lost much earlier – in 1946 and 1947 when Bevin's desire for a customs union had been thwarted by the Treasury and the Board of Trade. That apart, it was this kind of thinking amongst the Western Europeans which was to be given institutional shape in the ECSC and, more so, the EEC.

What is at issue here, therefore, is not the greater foresight of the Europeans compared to the policymakers of Britain in this period. These were trends which are more clearly decipherable from our vantage point than they were at the time. Even when changes in economic patterns were detected there was no telling whether they would be permanent. As Milward points out, 'what became all too visible by 1960 was only just perceptible in 1950 and certainly anything but irreversible' (p. 361). The integrationists were, one might say, fortunate in that they were buoyed up and carried along by these trends. The British, consulting other auguries which seemed no less reliable, were proved wrong. Two years after the war Britain exported five times as much as France and as much as all the future Six put together. Her GDP in 1950 was twice that of either France or Germany. Despite (possibly temporary) setbacks, her foreign trade and her industrial output were still in 1951 as large as those of France and Germany combined and she was responsible for a third of the industrial production of all the OEEC countries (Cairncross, 1985, p. 278). For better or worse, the bulk of British exports went outside Europe. Officials did not fail to attempt to draw lessons from all this. The originators of Plan G in 1956 noted that,

The European market has been increasing in importance in the last few years, for it has been expanding steadily at a time when the markets in primary-producing countries have been stagnant. But less than one-third of our trade is with Europe; entry into a common market would be bound to damage much of the other two-thirds (particularly that with the Commonwealth). This course would take us too far towards Europe. (quoted in Lamb, 1987, p. 92)

This was not necessarily unsound advice for a country which had for a century been more dependent on imports of foodstuffs than any of the states which were then opting for the EEC, and it is a reminder that the price of Britain's entry would have been high even if an early decision had been taken. The essential point is that 'in order to adjust to the EEC she had to uproot and replant, while her neighbours cultivated the fields they already had' (Porter, 1987, p. 125).

None the less, the fact remains that while Britain held back others made the leap towards union. This, inescapably, brings us back to her perception of herself in the world. Underlying everything was Britain's non-European tradition and that the altered circumstances which had now begun to undermine this were largely ignored. Indeed, it was the very rapidity with which change was even then taking place − in her economic position, amongst her colonial possessions and inside Europe itself − which made it less easy to assess it objectively. Britain in 1955 continued to be a significant economic power with worldwide prestige and influence and with a long tradition of political stability. Neither France nor Germany could make such claims. Aside from the underlying economic imperatives towards integration, the events of 1940, plus the lack of political cohesion in the Fourth Republic and severe crises over Indo-China and Algeria, made it easier for France to take the leap, just as those of 1945, plus the relatively smooth transition from Empire to Commonwealth, made it harder for Britain. As for Germany, she wanted the status and respectability which association with her Western neighbours would bring and was prepared to give up a good deal in order to achieve this.

It remains debatable, also whether, Britain could, in 1955/56, have entered the EEC on more favourable terms than she was to obtain in 1973. The French by a mixture of skilful tactics and bloody-mindedness − a refusal, for instance, to approve the Spaak Report at the Venice Conference unless arrangements were made to associate the French colonies with the customs union − were able to obtain a

75

whole catalogue of special arrangements. It is unlikely that such leverage was available to the British, even had they attempted to bring it to bear. The fact was that France was indispensable to the customs union and Britain, with her trading pattern still peripheral to Europe, was not. It is worth recalling here that supranationality was toned down in the Spaak Report as much to entice the French as to attempt to appease the British. Also French weaknesses turned out to be strengths. Spaak's recurring fears that the current French Government might fall to be replaced by one with less European sympathies helped condition him to fall in with their demands. Moreover, concessions related to the French colonies were more straightforward than would have been the case with the Commonwealth. It was a matter of scale. The Ivory Coast was not New Zealand, Gabon was not Australia and association between these and the EEC was unlikely to tilt the economic community severely in France's favour.

It cannot be denied, nevertheless, that the British, by distancing themselves from European developments over the previous five or six years, had signally contributed to their own marginalization. What was so different about the negotiations surrounding the EEC was that for the first time since 1945 the British opened themselves to the charge of being actively hostile and destructive towards integration. Until then they had tempered their aloofness with a blend of goodwill towards European projects and a desire to be 'associated' with them. During 1956 the hope of influencing developments towards a free trade association easily slid into a deliberate attempt to wreck the customs union project which the Europeans were increasingly showing a determination to pursue. This was a most significant change. In the short term it produced a series of blunders — joining the Spaak Committee and then withdrawing, attempting to induce the Americans and the Germans to disrupt Spaak's progress, inaugurating the Free Trade Area as a means of spoiling the EEC — which only made the British position worse. More seriously, the change of strategy was indicative of a Power which had begun to glimpse that it was heading down a *cul de sac*. It dawned, sporadically, during 1956 that the French and Germans might well set up a customs union and that, if this happened, Britain could not to afford to stay out (Lamb, 1987, p. 91; Young, 1989, p. 205). They remained, nevertheless, almost paralyzed in the face of the challenge.

The thinking, and the prejudices, which produced this were encapsulated in the attitudes of Anthony Eden. As Foreign Secretary and, from April 1955, Prime Minister, the tone which he set was inevitably significant. His main preoccupation was adjustments which would maintain Britain's world position as leader of the Commonwealth and joint leader of the Western World. Until the climacteric of the Suez Crisis in 1956 (which, of course, took up most of his time during crucial EEC negotiations) he had shown some competence in doing this. Europe did not interest him, other than as the vague source of Western civilization and as a means of consolidating Western defences. As for integration, according to R. A. Butler, Eden 'was bored with this. Frankly he was even more bored than I was' (Charlton, 1983, pp. 172–3, 195). This may seem somewhat perverse in the light of Eden's 'Atlanticism' and the known American enthusiasm for federalism. But even if it was clear, – and Washington seems to have been erratic over this – that the United States viewed Britain as a part of an integrated Europe, Eden judged it incompatible with a 'special relationship' on which transatlantic bridge-building was founded. Besides, Eden was frequently inclined to resist what he regarded as the more excessive policies of the United States if only to emphasize Britain's independent global role.

In the final analysis, Eden's stance was no different from those colleagues whose ministerial positions put them in closer range of European events during this period and some of whom were later to profess long-standing 'European' sympathies. Butler, Chancellor of the Exchequer at the time of the re-launch, brushed aside the Messina conference as 'archaeological excavations' and seems to have been influenced in his dismissal of the initiative by his 'repugnance' for Beyen, 'a very pushing man ... always telling you what to do' (Charlton, 1983, pp. 190, 194). Butler's role in creating a feeling of intense irritation towards the British on the part of Beyen and Spaak at a sensitive point in negotiations seems to have been crucial. Selwyn Lloyd, who took over from Macmillan as Foreign Secretary at the end of 1955, facetiously described the debate over the common market as 'much ado about nothing' (Lamb, 1987, p. 91). Maudling, from August 1957 chairing the committee which hoped to build a partnership between a free trade area and the Six, was not beyond demonstrating an open lack of sympathy for the objectives of Britain's prospective associates (Camps, 1964, p. 168). Thorneycroft, President of the Board of Trade throughout the Eden Government, has cultivated a reputation as a 'pro-European'. Yet he was among the first to urge Bretherton's withdrawal from the Spaak Committee. When it looked increasingly likely that a customs union might emerge he swung his support round to Plan G. In this he was supported by Macmillan. As

Foreign Secretary, Macmillan had, like Eden before him, concentrated on areas other than Europe. After becoming Chancellor in December 1955 he pushed for the acceptance of Plan G. Despite his apparent optimism that this could succeed, the low esteem in which he held the OEEC – the basis of the Plan – and the determination that he would 'not be bullied' by the Six, suggest that behind the trappings of a modest conversion to 'Europeanism' lay nothing much more than a common British reflex urge to wreck the Spaak proposals. There were, indeed, for more or less understandable reasons, no real 'pro-Europeans' in the Eden Government.

7

Squaring the Circles, 1958−67

Harold Macmillan's announcement in the summer of 1961 that Britain intended to apply for full membership of the EEC appears less remarkable thirty years on than it did at the time. It is now apparent that even as EFTA was being set up the spark of recognition existed that this was a false trail. A cluster of political and economic developments in the late fifties and early sixties confirmed this. Macmillan's decision, however, was not founded on a conviction that such signals implied any radical departure from the past. What was required, rather, was a new political and economic base which would underpin Britain's existing world role: that base would be Europe. The decision to 'join Europe', therefore, had nothing to do with federalism and 'hardly constituted a new departure by the British, but should be seen rather as a means of restoring Britain to her old position at the intersection of the three circles − Europe, America and the Commonwealth' (Sked and Cook, 1990, pp. 168−9).

Since the war, a dozen former imperial possessions in Asia and Africa had been given independence. This process of decolonization was still gaining momentum. Transformation from Empire to Commonwealth, while something of a moral victory for Britain, was politically enervating. Common ground between 'third world' black nations and a highly industrialized white power was not always easy to find and there was little inclination on the part of the former to continue the deferential ways of the past. Patchy Commonwealth support for Britain during the Suez Crisis in 1956 and the decision, against British instincts, to eject South Africa from the Commonwealth in 1961 both, in their different ways, demonstrated that Britain was not fully master in the house she had constructed.

Suez also indicated in a most public fashion that the supposed 'special relationship' with the United States, the power most responsible for Britain's loss of face in that crisis, was a rather one-sided affair. This imbalance had always been implicit in America's towering economic superiority over Britain since 1945. The hope had been that this would be evened out by Britain's political experience. She would, to paraphrase Harold Macmillan, play the role of the refined Greeks to America's less sophisticated Romans, leading them in careful partnership to take actions which suited British purposes. But even before Suez the Americans had shown an irritating refusal to play the role the British had assigned them. Common interests between the two in the Cold War ensured that good relations would rapidly be restored after the rift in 1956, but it was becoming increasingly difficult to maintain the fiction that this was a partnership of equals.

The year in which Harold Macmillan succeeded the ailing Eden as Prime Minister, 1957, saw the launch of the Soviet space satellite, 'Sputnik'. The frightening military implications of this achievement were to galvanize the Americans and lead to the successful space programme of the 1960s. The British also were spurred into action, though the results were considerably less spectacular. The development of a rocket, Blue Streak, as the means of delivering the British nuclear deterrent was authorized, only to be cancelled within three years because of escalating costs. Though Macmillan's procurement of an American alternative to Blue Streak from Eisenhower in the shape of Skybolt might be taken as evidence of the continuation of the 'special relationship', the fact remained that Britain's membership of the 'Nuclear Club' now depended, in the last resort, on Washington (Sanders, 1990, pp. 172−3). It may be that, for Macmillan, the real symbol of Britain's dwindling world influence came at the East−West summit meeting in May 1960 (Horne, 1989, p. 256). Undoubtedly the Prime Minister was the impresario of the summit, hoping to see Britain play the leading role in cooling world tensions. Two weeks before the Paris gathering, however, an American U-2 spy plane was shot down over Soviet territory and the summit disintegrated before it had begun revealing, once more, British impotence in the face of wrangles between the Superpowers. Though the Soviet Union was ultimately responsible for this collapse, it was the fluctuating relations with the Americans − with, as Macmillan complained, Britain 'treated now as just another country, now as an ally in a special and unique category' − which caused most concern (quoted in Bartlett, 1977, p. 188). Europe increasingly came to be seen as the avenue through which the Anglo-American relationship might be stabilized. Even before the summit setback, Macmillan had set up an interdepartmental committee of senior civil servants chaired by Sir Frank Lee, Permanent Secretary at the Treasury, to re-examine Britain's relationship with the Six (Camps, 1964, p. 280).

Washington's continuing sympathy towards European integration and dismay that Britain felt unable to play a full part in the process was an important element in this shift. The Eisenhower Administration had tended to dismiss ideas of British 'association' with the EEC and the decision to form EFTA as unneccessary complications. Such conflicts of view on Europe between London and Washington had not mattered so much when the disparity in power between the two had been less obvious. Britain's dependence on the Americans for their nuclear capability, and therefore, implicitly, for her continuing status as a Great Power, had put a different complexion on things by the early sixties. There were growing fears too that if Britain did not redefine her attitude towards Europe she would be bypassed by the United States, who would work more closely with the Europeans. Such considerations were presumably in the forefront of the minds of those civil servants who had been instructed by Macmillan to review Britain's stance; and their conclusions favouring Britain's joining the EEC were founded principally on political considerations. The United States, it was argued, would look increasingly to the Community as its main partner in the West. Outside this grouping, Britain would surely lose influence. The best way of reasserting the balance in Britain's favour would be to join the EEC. This 'seems to have been a very important – perhaps the controlling – element in Mr. Macmillan's own decision that the right course for the United Kingdom was to apply for membership' (Camps, 1964, pp. 281, 336). When Kennedy, who succeeded Eisenhower as President in 1961, personally assured Macmillan in April of that year that a move to join the Six would be welcomed by him and might well lead to a closer Anglo-American relationship, it provided Macmillan with gratifying support for a route which he had already decided to take (Horne, 1989, p. 295).

Yet economic factors were also crucial and were to be central to the domestic debate over the next two decades and beyond. Indeed, economic and political considerations were knotted together. The Community threatened to become a political rival to a Britain trapped outside it precisely because it was proving economically successful. American investment which had formerly gone to Britain was already being diverted to the EEC (Northedge, 1974, p. 337). An economically stagnant EEC would have changed nothing. It was the growing recognition in London that the Community was working which was fundamental to everything that followed. This included depressing comparisons between the vigour of certain Western European economies and British economic growth which, though statistically encouraging, was less dynamic than that achieved by her continental neighbours. Recurring balance-of-payments crises were met by a frustrating cycle of measures taken first to promote demand and then to damp it down so as to stem the alarming flood of imports which stimulation had produced.

What was not clear, however, was whether being a member of the Six would provide the key to economic vitality. While indices for the EEC as a whole were impressive, Belgium, inside the Community, performed less well than Britain, whereas Austria, outside it, performed better. Nor was there any certainty that entry into Europe would resolve the problem of Britain's economic sluggishness; for the causes of that might rest too deeply in structures and practices inherent in the British system (Sanders, 1990, pp. 143−4). On the other hand, here was a market of 170 million people to which Britain had only limited access. There was also the possibility, an argument stressed by Macmillan's interdepartmental committee, that exposure to this marketplace might, in itself, serve to shake out some of the domestic impediments to British economic progress. No one, on the other hand, had any faith that membership of EFTA could ease these difficulties. What was more exactly measurable was the developing shift in Britain's post-war trade. This was, by the end of the fifties, noticeably away from Empire and Commonwealth and towards Europe (Kitzinger, 1973, p. 28). Unwittingly and largely unnoticed, Britain was moving more emphatically into the European 'circle'. In this sense, there was an inevitability about Britain's entry into Europe, and 'whatever the express calculations of the decision makers themselves, (it was) merely the response of a political system trying to catch up with economic realities' (Sanders, 1990, p. 156).

Association rather than membership, however, had been Macmillan's initial objective. He had made positive attempts to strengthen political links with the Six, which had significantly deteriorated during the EFTA negotiations, through meetings of the Council of Europe and WEU, with the idea of developing some form of customs union with the EEC. In June 1960 guarded hints were dropped that Britain might be ready to take the half-way house of joining the ECSC and

Euratom. It came to nothing. Britain, Monnet admonished, must 'decide to join the whole procession ... and not a piece of it, leaving the rest aside' (quoted in Camps, 1964, p. 291). By now, Macmillan was coming to this conclusion too. To the weight of the larger political and economic arguments for joining the Community were added more pressing considerations. Tariff cuts within the EEC were progressing at a much faster rate than had been envisaged by the Treaty of Rome, and Community negotiations on agricultural policy were also ahead of schedule. De Gaulle, who many had believed would decelerate the impetus of the European movement, had, in fact, begun to forge closer contacts with Adenauer's Germany and to talk of common political initiatives among the Six. The sooner Britain joined, the sooner she would have a say in these developments.

In some ways the situation was working in Britain's favour. De Gaulle's view of Europe coming together in a cooperative confederation of nation states rather than in a future supranational United States of Europe was much more acceptable to Britain than the objectives of the federalists. It was an enormous advantage for succeeding British governments not to have to concentrate on the potentially destructive issue of sovereignty, as had been the case in the 1950s, in selling membership of the Community to a wider British audience. Somewhat paradoxically, it was alarm over de Gaulle's views which moved his partners among the Six to provide a counterbalance to France by encouraging Britain to join them. The first to do so, in the summer of 1960, was Adenauer, followed rapidly by the Italians. De Gaulle himself also seemed to indicate that he was ready to accommodate the British.

A common theme in British conversations with the European governments in the middle of 1960, however, was that there would be no half measures. Britain must seek full membership of the EEC or nothing. (Kennedy seems to have implied the same when he met Macmillan in April of the next year.) Probably it was this new mood, rather than the failure of the 1960 summit, which provided the real turning point. Macmillan spoke of his talks with Adenauer in the summer of 1960 as 'historic'. According to Heath, 'It was on the results of that that the Prime Minister decided it was timely to make an application to join the Community' (quoted in Charlton, 1983, p. 243). 'European-minded' Ministers were now placed in strategic governmental positions – Sandys at the Commonwealth Office, Soames at the Ministry of Agriculture and Heath as Foreign Office Minister with a particular brief for Europe. Armed with the conclusions of the Lee Committee report – which indicated that for the first time in over fifteen years the Treasury and the Board of Trade were not to be a dead weight on closer economic links with Europe – Macmillan now sought to persuade the Cabinet and the country.

Signs that the Government was on the point of a change of policy even before the announcement on 31 July 1961 of the intention to apply for membership of the EEC, meant that the national debate on Britain's role in Europe had already begun. It was to continue almost without interruption into the nineties. A potent centre of opposition within the Conservative Party was likely to revolve around the natural uncertainties of industrialists, businessmen and farmers about radical change. Concern to protect these interest groups was a central consideration in the negotiations which were soon to take place. More predictable was obstruction from the right of the Party, where there remained many who resented the idea of submerging Britain's national and imperial past by joining what some still referred to as 'a collection of losers' (Charlton, 1983, p. 241). This may account for Macmillan's emphasis on political considerations in his announcement in the Commons, as an attempt to appease the Tory right by stressing the dangers of isolation while temporarily glossing over economic issues.

In fact, the right failed to carry the Party with them and the Party Conference in October gave clear support for the Government's decision. The Labour Party Conference, on the other hand, did not. Here the views most vociferously promoted by the left, that the EEC was a conservative, Catholic, 'capitalist club' which would hinder the objectives of socialism in Britain if she joined, triumphed, and though there was strong support for joining amongst certain members of the Labour leadership and in the moderate-left press, the Party's stance remained negative. The press, on the whole, was favourable to EEC membership. This fact probably goes some way to explaining a moderate popular inclination to support entry as reflected in opinion polls. (This was to decline once negotiations got under way.) All this allowed Macmillan to win over the waverers in his Cabinet, though there was not complete unanimity until some time after negotiations for entry had actually begun (Kitzinger, 1973, p. 352).

Negotiations were inevitably long and complex. Discussing ways and means of joining an economic community which had already begun to firm up its own rules and practices presented obvious problems. Sovereignty continued to rumble as a domestic issue, but was not an overt agenda item in the Brussels talks. None the less, the most significant areas of contention were ones which had sprung from Britain's particular historical experience and were not open to

84

simple solutions. Two of these were linked. Although not self-sufficient in foodstuffs, the British were used to cheap food prices because of Britain's efficient, subsidized farming and, more so, because of preferential trading arrangements with the Commonwealth. A common EEC agricultural policy which was actually being thrashed out as negotiations on British entry proceeded would inevitably mean the end of government subsidies and increased competition. Though the British system was ripe for overhaul anyway, these remained not insignificant considerations, affecting as they might the potential well-being of a class which made up a significant part of the British political establishment and of the Conservative Party in particular. However, 'the Commonwealth aspects of the question overshadowed all others, politically, economically and emotionally' (Camps, 1964, p. 338). Not only would observance of the common internal tariff mean an end to thirty years of preference, there was severe concern whether the Commonwealth as an entity could actually survive such a shift. Hence the British concern to find a way of reducing the effects of dislocation for those Commonwealth countries which were heavily dependent upon Britain for a market for their exports. These included the raw materials of Nigeria and Sierra Leone, though it was New Zealand lamb and butter which tended to grab the limelight. Added to all this, Britain's more recent partners in EFTA had to be cast adrift without too obvious signs of scuttle.

But negotiations on these key issues never reached a natural conclusion. At a press conference on 14 January 1963, General de Gaulle declared Britain unfit for membership. 'England', de Gaulle stated,

is, in effect, insular ... In short, the nature and structure and economic context of England differ profoundly from those of the other states of the Continent ... In the end there would appear a colossal Atlantic community under American dependence and leadership which would soon swallow up the European Community. (quoted in Horne, 1989, p. 446)

Heath, the chief British negotiator, attempted to continue as though nothing had happened. At first, France's partners, most of whom were incensed by de Gaulle's cavalier and unilateral action, seemed prepared to go along with this fiction, but in the end, unwilling to risk mortal damage to the Community itself, they fell into line with the French. By February Britain's first attempt to enter the European Community had come to an end.

De Gaulle's action still rankles with many who write of it. To some it had come deliberately just as the negotiations were reaching break-through (Bartlett, 1977, p. 193; George, 1990, p. 35; Mowat, 1973, p. 170; Northedge, 1974, p. 346; Sanders, 1990, p. 139). The most detailed study of these negotiations, however, presents a more cautious assessment, arguing that without de Gaulle's intervention, agreement was likely though 'the problems outstanding were ... potentially rather more troublesome than some of the statements made by Mr. Macmillan and Mr. Heath seemed to suggest.' These included a future accommodation with New Zealand and with Britain's EFTA partners. Thus, 'any judgement on what might have been is hazardous' (Camps, 1964, pp. 493, 506).

The motive for de Gaulle's veto must also remain a matter for speculation. The suggestion that he had never wanted British membership, and had smiled on a British application only when there seemed little chance of its success and then become alarmed by the smoothness of the negotiations, tends to gloss over the real difficulties which still had to be resolved and the acrimony which these engendered not only between Britain and France but between Britain and all the Six (Willis, 1968, p. 303). It may be, rather, that he genuinely sought British membership but that the British negotiating position, and other events during 1962, caused him to change his mind. This is the interpretation favoured by the chief British negotiator at the time, Edward Heath (Charlton, 1983, p. 280). The similarity between the majority British view and the Gaullist view on Europe provides further corroboration. Both were suspicious of supranationalism and envisaged cooperation developing on an inter-governmental rather than a feder-alist level. At the time of his announcement of Britain's intention to seek membership of the Community, Macmillan made a point of publicly declaring his agreement with the Gaullist concept of a '*Europe des patries*'. This apparent common ground may have allowed the Prime Minister the illusion that he could handle de Gaulle. It was a mirage. While the stance of each was similar, the reasons for adopting it were significantly different. The British rejected supranationalism because they feared a long-term loss of parliamentary sovereignty to the 'faceless bureaucrats' of Brussels and because they still held ambitions to play a leading role on a wider world stage; de Gaulle rejected it because of the more immediate threat it posed to the French leadership of Europe.

In fact, de Gaulle's especial attitude towards European cooperation had been understood for some time. In some ways it was reminiscent of Bevin's ideas in the 1940s, in that de Gaulle wished to see the development of a European power-bloc which could stand its own ground against the two Superpowers. The driving force behind this objective was a strong sense of nationalism enhanced by France's wartime humiliations and reinforced by the crises over Suez (1956) and Cuba (1962), each of which, in its own way, had demonstrated the ebbing of European power. The federalism of Monnet and the 'Europeans' was, for de Gaulle, not the answer. As well as being impractical it implied the submersion of France in an entity which would itself be merely the creature of its main patron – the United States. In de Gaulle's scheme of things, Europe would be guided by a strong France, armed with its own nuclear capability, the *force de frappe*, and weaned away from the American-dominated system of NATO.

There were obvious dangers in such a messianic view. But it was, in its own way, 'pro-European', and not necessarily inconsistent with British membership of the Community. It was true, however, that Britain would need to undergo a profound reorientation in her external relations if she were to be an acceptable partner to France. From at least mid-1962, de Gaulle was unconvinced that this was taking place. This, no doubt, involved a number of hard-headed and quite pragmatic considerations. French trade with Commonwealth countries was insignificant. It would be no enrichment to the French economy to accede to British demands for special considerations for the Commonwealth. On the contrary, it might damage French economic interests by giving advantage not only to the British but also to the Germans, who did have significant trading links with the Commonwealth (Willis, 1968, pp. 300–1). The same was true of agriculture. Here Britain's special pleading might well endanger the recently agreed common policy which markedly favoured French farmers.

Though these were clearly nationalistic considerations they were also connected to de Gaulle's view of Europe and France's place within it. On a broader level, a form of 'association' with the Commonwealth threatened not only to tilt the balance of influence towards the British but also to dilute the very cohesion of the community which he wished to create. The same was true of any special arrangements for EFTA. Though some EFTA members were now interested in full EEC membership, there were the formally neutral – Austria, Sweden and Switzerland – who felt unable to do so. The uncommitted connection which these countries sought was unpalatable. Above all, it was Britain's role as champion of these 'outsiders' plus frequent British assertions that membership of the EEC involved no element of 'choice' between Europe and Commonwealth which suggested that application to join was not going to be a profound break with tradition. A variable, essentially noncommittal, public opinion in Britain coupled with opposition within the Labour Party, increasingly seen as the likely next British Government, served only to reinforce this view.

The real problem, however, was the Anglo-American connection. The concept of the three intersecting circles looked even more lopsided from Paris than from London. Like the federalists, the British would allow Washington to dominate Europe. Proof that Britain was not prepared to loosen her ties with the United States and commit herself wholeheartedly to the Six came at the end of 1962 in the shape of a crisis over Britain's independent nuclear capability.

As mentioned earlier, Britain's inability to afford the development costs of the Blue Streak rockets had led Eisenhower to promise, in return for the use of Scottish bases for US nuclear submarines, American Skybolt missiles which were currently being tested. The tests failed and in December 1962, while British negotiations with the EEC were taking place, the Kennedy Administration informed London that the Skybolt programme was to be scrapped, leaving Britain without a delivery system for her hydrogen bombs. This glaring hole in Britain's pretensions to be a self-sufficient nuclear power overshadowed a meeting between Macmillan and de Gaulle held at Rambouillet, outside Paris, on 15–16 December. Here, the Prime Minister intimated that he would seek the Polaris submarine-delivered nuclear system from Kennedy, and it may have been this which finally turned de Gaulle decisively against British application to join the EEC. On the other hand, it was far from certain that the Americans would agree to supply Polaris, and scepticism may have allowed de Gaulle to believe for a short while that the outcome of this crisis would be to push Britain towards Europe (Horne, 1989, p. 431). This did not happen. Surprisingly, at a meeting with Kennedy at Nassau between 18 and 21 December, Macmillan persuaded the President to provide Britain with Polaris missiles. De Gaulle's press-conference veto followed in January.

It is not, of course, possible entirely to rule out baser motives for de Gaulle's action. However, a mixture of pique, resentment, chauvinism and arrogance as an explanation of the actions of this complex character runs the risk of falling into the same trap of narrow nationalism that de Gaulle is often accused of. Significantly, Edward Heath has suggested that there was a wider vision behind de Gaulle's European policy; he is not convinced either that the French President merely used the Skybolt issue as a convenient excuse to break off negotiations between Britain and the Six or that his intention was French domination, as opposed to leadership, of the Community (Charlton, 1983, pp. 298–9).

Moreover, de Gaulle's central assertion, that Britain was not yet ready to join the Community, in the sense that her preoccupations remained essentially extra-European, seems difficult to deny. Evidence for this existed from the start. Most commentators, for instance, have noted the lacklustre and unenthusiastic tone of Macmillan's announcement in July 1961 that he intended to apply for membership. The string of guarantees that was then sought also aroused suspicions, and not only among Gaullists, giving 'the impression of being a potential benefactor rather than a supplicant' (Urwin, 1989, p. 212). This, of course, may have had something to do with laying down a negotiating position, with Macmillan underplaying a significant change of direction until he had won over Cabinet, Party and country, and with Heath bidding high prior to a retreat to a mutually acceptable position. It is also true that the negotiating process was immensely complicated: Heath, having to deal with each of the Six separately while they, at the same time, were negotiating with each other over a common agricultural policy, likened it to negotiating on a 'moving belt'. There were also simultaneous discussions with the Commonwealth, with EFTA and with the US. The need to speak in a different voice to each of these audiences, stressing for instance to Commonwealth leaders that it was not a matter of opting for them or for Europe yet trying to assure the Six that Britain was now a committed European, inevitably produced ambiguities and reinforced the views of those Europeans who suspected that Britain continued to want the best of all worlds.

Yet this was indeed what she wanted. While the commercial and economic advantages of joining the Six remained marginal, the political advantages were significant – but only if gains were made without shedding existing influential attachments. 'We never went in to get something out,' the then Head of the British Foreign Office has since admitted. 'We went in to prevent our being kicked down really to a lower league' (quoted in Charlton, 1983, p. 304). Because this was the thinking, 'to a great extent the EEC was still seen rather as an addition to Britain's relations with the Commonwealth, and indeed with the United States, than as an alternative' (Bartlett, 1977,

p. 190). And, as de Gaulle realized, America was the linchpin; for, 'if Macmillan was ready to draw closer to Europe in economic terms, he remained unconvinced that such involvement should in any way prejudice London's close military and political relationship with Washington' (Sanders, 1990, p. 139).

This produced the enormous misjudgement on Macmillan's part that the Nassau deal would have no impact on the EEC negotiations, an error of judgement compounded by the fact that Macmillan was aware weeks before January that a French veto was likely and that an offer of Anglo-French nuclear collaboration might prevent it (Horne, 1989, p. 328). Moreover, Nassau underlined de Gaulle's case even more than the French President probably realized. At that meeting, Kennedy offered the British the chance to take over the Skybolt programme. It would mean continued dependence on the Americans for their nuclear armoury but less so than would Polaris. None the less, Macmillan pressed for Polaris.

But the miscalculation was Kennedy's also. Recent accounts suggest a more concerted Anglo-American assault on the leadership of the Community and that

> In effect, Macmillan seems to have been responding to consistent
> US advocacy of British membership, 'to go in there and dominate
> it on behalf of joint British and American concerns'. This was
> precisely what de Gaulle suspected the British of attempting
> to do, and was the grounds for his veto. (George, 1990,
> pp. 39–40)

Macmillan's official biographer also implies the existence, since the first Kennedy-Macmillan meeting in April 1961, of an Anglo-American understanding to wrest the leadership of Europe away from the French (Horne, 1989, p. 295). What does seem quite clearly to be the case is that addiction to the supposed 'special relationship' was both a prime catalyst of Britain's first application to join the EEC and the major cause of what Macmillan called a 'great and grievous disappointment . . . at the end of a fine vision' (Horne, 1989, p. 448).

Disappointment was to continue, and a second bid to join the European Community ('EC', since the formal merger of ECSC, Euratom and EEC in 1965) was again vetoed by de Gaulle in May 1967. This time the application came from Harold Wilson's Labour Government, which had been in office since 1964. Wilson's decision to apply for membership demonstrated a shift of ground equal to that of Macmillan's in the early sixties. Ever since Ernest Bevin's European schemes had turned to dust and been outpaced by the Monnet-Schuman initiatives, the Labour Party had turned its face against European cooperation and, no less then the Conservatives, emphasized Atlantic and Commonwealth relations as the main planks of Britain's external relations. As a member of the Opposition, Wilson, like the majority of Labour supporters, had been vehemently hostile to the Heath negotiations in Brussels. Now, after three years in office, he pressed a hesitant Party back to the negotiating table. The fact that two Labour Foreign Secretaries at this time, Michael Stuart and George Brown, had become firm proponents of British entry was no doubt an influence upon Wilson. Brown, in particular, had adopted the earlier Bevinite position that an EC expanded to include Britain might 'stop the polarisation of the world around the two superpowers' (George-Brown, 1972, p. 133).

Ultimately, however, economics were at the heart of this change, and economic considerations dominated all others in this latest attempt by the British to prise entrance into what, perhaps significantly, was colloquially termed 'the Common Market'. The balance-of-payments problem remained as intractable under Labour as under the Conservatives and 'the story of the years 1964−67 was in large part the story of Labour's desperate attempts − in the end unavailing − to avoid having to devalue the pound' (King, 1977, p. 13). The consequent continuation of 'stop−go' policies meant that British economic growth was significantly lower than any member of the EC. Few now saw trade with the Commonwealth as a solution to Britain's difficulties. Indeed, earlier negotiations with the EEC had helped condition both sides to acknowledge the change in economic relationship between Britain and the Commonwealth as a matter of fact. Increasingly, the wider market of the Six was seen as the means by which Britain could participate in what Wilson called the 'white-hot technological revolution', and resentment over being 'dictated to by foreigners' gave way to warnings of becoming the 'economic helots' of American multinational companies. Such thinking raised questions about the 'special relationship' which had flourished under Macmillan. So too did devaluation when it finally came at the end of 1967. Among other things, devaluation speeded up plans to withdraw defence commitments east of Suez and to concentrate resources in Europe and the North Atlantic. To the American Defense Department this signified that the British 'are no longer a powerful ally of ours because they cannot afford the cost of an adequate defense effort' (quoted in Warner, 1989, p. 495).

De Gaulle's determination to create a confederation of states and to thwart the EC Commission's pretensions to power, which he had ruthlessly succeeded in doing during 1965, marginalized the issue of political integration and therefore made it easier for the Labour Government to come to terms with the idea of membership. What was now at issue was the ability of Britain to compete in an advanced industrial world with the markets, resources and research which were available to the US and the EC. Linked with this was the continuing fear that economic stagnation would inevitably lead to political isolation with Britain not at the intersection of three circles but in no circle at all. Under Wilson, as under his predecessor,

> There was no conversion to the ideal of European union that was espoused by the leaders of the founder states; there was no attempt to sell the idea of British membership in anything other than pragmatic terms to the British electorate; there was no abandonment at either official or popular level of a commitment to a strong sense of national identity ... there was no abandonment of the attachment to the special relationship with the United States, or of the commitment at both official and popular levels to the Atlantic Alliance as the basis of international stability. (George, 1990, p. 40).

Not himself a natural supporter of European cooperation and fully aware of the problems in presenting a *volte face* on Europe to Cabinet and Party, Wilson at first havered. His initial inclination was to promote, as had Bevin, Eden and Macmillan before him, some form of association between EFTA and the EC, or between the EC and Britain. Even after this had been abandoned as impracticable, it was far from clear that de Gaulle would now smile upon a British application for full membership. Indeed, early in 1967, both Wilson and Brown were told in an otherwise encouraging tour of Western European capitals preparatory to application that, so far as the French were concerned, little had changed (Shlaim, Jones and Sainsbury, 1977, p. 212). Hope seems to have rested on support for the British case from the other EC states. So, notwithstanding a divided Cabinet and with dissension in the Party, the British application was tabled in July 1967. In November, de Gaulle rejected it, repeating his assertion that Britain was not yet ready for membership. This time he laid stress upon British economic weakness, and it may be that fears that the new member might be an economic liability swayed Britain's erstwhile supporters in the Community against her. In any case, the fact remained that however difficult a partner France might be, she was more important a member of the EC than Britain. Moreover, despite British protestations, 'De Gaulle's analysis of Britain's predicament, if it contained a personal element, had more truth than it was customary to concede' (Robbins, 1983, p. 263).

8

Into Europe, 1967–75

Britain's entry into the European Community on 1 January 1973 was, on the popular level, extraordinarily anti-climatical for such an historic turning-point. The mood in Britain was 'reluctant, almost resigned', and 'the main feeling that determined public attitudes was that Britain's economic weakness was so endemic and prolonged that exclusion from a growing European market would be dangerous, almost fatal' (Morgan, 1990, p. 340). Ever since membership of the EC had become an issue under Macmillan, public opinion had oscillated more or less between hostility and indifference. This may have had something to do with a perception of entry on the crude level as a contest between Britain and de Gaulle and one in which the odds were, temporarily, stacked against them. More fundamentally, it was a matter which seemed remote from the daily lives of the average British citizen, and 'most voters knew little about Europe and cared less. The cost of living, unemployment, and strikes were issues for "us" — concrete, personal, and likely to have a direct bearing on the lives of individuals. Europe by contrast was an issue for "them" — a politicians' issue, abstract, remote, having little bearing on daily life' (King, 1977, p. 26).

Neither of the two major political parties had done much to try to alter such attitudes. Europe was not a contentious electoral issue and the parties preferred to lead rather than educate even when, as at the start of the successful 1973 negotiations, public opinion was significantly anti-European. While this was, arguably, an admirable trait in a mature democracy, it harboured real dangers. Fissures within both parties were glossed over and the full implications of membership of a potentially federal European Community were never clearly laid out to the British people. Indeed, 'what was lacking throughout, as in Britain's approach towards the concept of European unity since the days of the Schuman Plan in 1950, was a head-on engagement with the issues of principle involved in attaching Britain to a wider entity and breaking down centuries of insularity' (Morgan, 1990, p. 363).

After the second veto of 1967 the Labour Government had left the British application on the table to be picked up when de Gaulle had left the scene. Only the surprise defeat of the Labour Government in the General Election of 1970 prevented it from doing this and the Labour Party from being able to lay claim, as the Conservatives are prone, to being the true 'Party of Europe'. Not Wilson, but his successor as Prime Minister, Edward Heath, earned the credit of being the man who took Britain into Europe. This, at least, was fitting; for while the Conservative Party was to demonstrate a proclivity almost equal to that of Labour to descend into discord over Britain's role in Europe, Heath's credentials as a pro-European and his luke-warm attitude towards the 'special relationship' were greater than any Premier in the post-war period. It may also have been the case that the understanding which developed between Heath and Georges Pompidou, de Gaulle's successor, helped remove lingering doubts which remained in the Gaullist camp about British membership.

Heath was undoubtedly strongly motivated by the ideals of a tightly bound community – wherever they might lead. Also, like Macmillan before him, he hoped the thrust into a more competitive environment would purge the British economy of archaic attitudes and practices which had been a dead hand since the end of the war. Promises of future prosperity, rather than appeals to European idealism, perhaps account for the distinct upswing in support for Britain's entry of the EC as the negotiations proceeded through 1971 and 1972 among a population which was not expected to think too deeply about the wider implications of what they were being asked to embark upon. Entry on this basis was almost certain to disappoint.

Heath's fervour for the European Idea turned out to be both an asset and something of a disadvantage. In the first place, there were enormous obstacles to overcome in order to achieve British membership and Heath's commitment was an important ingredient in triumphing over these. Once Britain was in the Community, however, the Prime Minister often appeared to be more European than many of his partners, who resented the newcomer's attempts to remould institutions which had functioned effectively without the British for almost two decades.

95

At the outset of the negotiations in the summer of 1970 Heath was faced with a public opinion which was adamantly against the process. Furthermore, almost immediately after losing power in the summer of 1970 the Labour Party had readopted a hostile stance towards entry to the EC. Throughout the period of negotiations with the Six the Labour Party condemned the Conservatives' terms of entry as unacceptable – although, had Wilson been in Heath's shoes, it seems improbable that the outcome would have been very different. To a certain degree the terms were distasteful to Labour simply because it was Heath and not Wilson who was negotiating them and therefore had to be opposed in the same way as had, say, the Government's Industrial Relations Bill. But the Party had also swung significantly to the left, and the left was the home of the most committed anti-Marketeers. More than this, the issue of Europe had riven the Party from top to bottom. In a parliamentary vote on the terms of entry on 28 October 1971, Wilson's rejection of the terms was defied by half his Shadow Cabinet. As one commentator has noted, '"Rebellion" is too weak a word for what happened on October 28. This was civil war' (King, 1977, p. 42). Wilson's urging of a policy of acceptance of the principle of EC membership while opposing the terms which were emerging at the negotiations in Luxembourg was no more than a precarious ploy to preserve Party unity. It was not a happy position and Wilson's discomfort came through in private complaints to his Labour colleagues that he had been 'wading in shit for three months to allow others to indulge their conscience' (Healey, 1990, p. 260).

Nor were the Conservatives united. A substantial minority of the parliamentary party voted against their own government in October 1971 and Heath was reliant upon Liberal and Labour support or abstentions. The same divisive pattern emerged in the closely fought struggle to pass the bill which provided the necessary legislation to take Britain into Europe and was voted into law in February 1972 by only eight votes. As has been pointed out, 'the conflict both within and between parties over Europe was by far the most serious foreign policy issue in British politics between 1970 and 1974. The parties might vary in degree in their attitudes to the American alliance, the Soviet Union and the United Nations, but their differences, between front benches at least, were rarely fundamental. The European question was the one which really roused passions' (Sked and Cook, 1990, p. 265).

On top of all this and despite Heath's good working relationship with Pompidou, and his friendship with the pro-British West German Chancellor, Willy Brandt, the terms of entry which he was able to obtain were unfavourable to Britain. Some of the real obstacles to British entry in the 1950s and 1960s had by this time largely evaporated. Supranationality, for instance, though implicit in the Treaty of Rome to which Britain now wished to accede, was, partly because economic issues had edged it aside and partly because of more pragmatic leadership in both Germany and France, left to hang as a muffled backdrop to the negotiations. Commonwealth issues had also subsided into questions of providing some safeguards for West Indian sugar producers and New Zealand dairy farmers. These proved contentious enough and were finally resolved by agreement to phase out Britain's preferential trade in these commodities over a four-year period. Far more problematical were matters arising from the development of the Community over twenty years or more and which Britain had now to fit in with.

The most difficult of these was the Common Agricultural Policy (CAP). This had been on the Community agenda from the early days of integration, promoted especially by the Dutch, who wished to protect the crucial agricultural sector of their economy, and by the French, who wished to ensure that those who worked in French agriculture should have a reasonable standard of living. It took some years to arrive at an agreed formula which would provide these sectional benefits, but by 1968 the CAP was providing a common market in agricultural products and a guaranteed return for farmers via the EC Commission's policy of buying surplus produce which had fallen below the annually stated price. It was certain that if Britain participated in such a system she would experience a significant increase in food prices. Yet there was little that Heath could do to alleviate this, given French resistance to concessions in this area and the status which the CAP had more generally among the six by this time as the most concrete sign that the Community was working successfully.

Added to this, the Community had agreed upon a formula in 1970 by which its budget would be based on revenues from agricultural products and industrial goods imported from outside the EC. As Britain imported more of both from beyond the Community than any other member state, she was likely to be one of the largest contributors to the budget. At the same time, she would gain little from the CAP on which most of the EC budget was spent. Although Heath was able to obtain a six-year transitional period before British contributions to the Community budget would reach their maximum, essentially his approach was 'to gain entry, and then sort out any difficulties' (George, 1990, p. 56). This was a perfectly understandable, even essential, approach but was to lead to enormous difficulties in the future.

Unfortunately, Britain's entry into the EC coincided with renewed economic problems. By the early 1970s the response of the United States to its own difficulties, a devaluation of the dollar and the raising of import duties, had produced an economic downturn on a world scale. The impact on Britain was an increase in both inflation and unemployment. This was made far worse by the decision of the Organization of Oil Exporting Countries (OPEC) to double the price of their prime source of revenue during, and again after, the Arab–Israeli war of 1972. These were inauspicious circumstances in which to convince domestic opinion, already becoming fearful of the personal cost, that the new European venture was to be welcomed.

Heath's expectation was that, in the long run, a shift in the pattern of British trade towards Europe would eventually reduce British liabilities to the Community budget and, hence, the cost of membership. More immediately, his intention was to persuade Britain's partners in the EC to create a European Regional Development Fund (ERDF) which would allow some concrete advantage from membership in the form of regional aid to the economically depressed areas of the United Kingdom and thus provide some counterweight to the disadvantages of agreeing to the CAP. Initial discussions on the size of the ERDF and how it should be distributed foundered on the economic problems which followed the energy crisis of 1973, and the Fund did not materialize until Heath had left office. Its future was uncertain even before this, however, because of resentment among the original Six, who felt that the British were not acting in a proper Community spirit. Whereas it was generally recognized that the setting up of an ERDF would be a positive move for the Community as a whole, it was also clear that it would be especially beneficial to British interests. This was acceptable so long as, in turn, Britain proved willing to support other developments which were less obviously advantageous to her. On a number of important issues, however, 'even Heath's Europeanism was selective' (Reynolds, 1991, p. 246). France and Germany were, at this point, keen to press forward with plans for Economic and Monetary Union (EMU) to which they had committed themselves before Britain joined the EC. But Britain refused to attach sterling to a joint float of European currencies which was a preliminary move towards EMU. This was particularly galling to the Germans who, because of their economic strength, would be expected to bear the greater proportion of the cost of the ERDF; and for them, 'the main justification for agreeing to it was as part of the price to keep the Community together; yet the British were not prepared to come together with the others on this important aspect of progress towards EMU' (George, 1990, p. 63). Well-intentioned, if sometimes undiplomatic, attempts by the British to increase the efficiency of the Community by urging that all its institutions be centred in Brussels, and open criticism of the Commission's handling of monetary policy, also served to annoy the original Six, who were affronted by such hectoring form the new boy. At the end of one year's membership and 'despite the good intentions of the Prime Minister, Britain had gained a reputation of being difficult to work with' (George, 1990, p. 70).

Progress towards EMU and the creation of the ERDF continued to be hampered by the severe implications of the international oil crisis. Under the impact of the crisis the forging of a joint energy policy became something of a test of Community solidarity. Here too the British demonstrated a capacity to be wayward. Before OPEC had precipitated the energy crisis by quadrupling oil prices during 1972–73, Heath had been a fervent proponent of a united policy on energy and, more particularly, of the idea that the EC should negotiate with the oil producers as an entity rather than as individuals. But the oil shortages resulting from the Arab–Israeli war of 1972 strengthened calls within the Community for regulation of internal distribution of oil supplies as the logical extension of the external policy which the British favoured. This was unacceptable to Britain on the familiar ground that it would mean an unnecessary extension of interference from Brussels. More significantly, the discovery of oil reserves in the North Sea meant that before long Britain would be self-sufficient in oil. This expectation was also to colour Labour's approach to Community energy policy on their return to power in 1974. While continuing to pay lip-service to the notion of a common European approach to world economic problems, the Labour Government, to the intense irritation of others in the EC, tried to insist that Britain's prospective status as an oil producer allowed her a separate voice to those of her partners when discussing world energy resources.

Labour's awkwardness was a particular source of dismay as the new Government had, by the end of 1975, seemed to resolve both its own and the nation's uncertainties about the EC and to be on the threshold of a more positive approach to Europe. As it turned out, the issue of British membership had not been settled either by the 1972 treaty or by Britain's formal entry into the EC in 1973. Instead the matter was damagingly prolonged. This was entirely to do with the return of a Labour Government in the General Election of February 1974. Neither of the two leading figures in the Labour Party, Harold Wilson and James Callaghan, felt much enthusiasm for the details of European integration, though both reluctantly recognized that Britain's long-term future lay in her continued membership of the EC. It has been said that 'for them, joining the Common Market was like getting up on a Monday morning; it was something one might have to do, but it was not something to get excited about' (King, 1977, p. 73). At the same time, they were presiding over a nation deeply divided after the domestic turmoil of the Heath Government, and over a party which was now predominantly anti-European but within which a significant core of fervent pro-Europeans remained. The priorities of the leadership, and of Wilson in particular, were to achieve a domestic consensus and to preserve party unity and then, if this could also be managed, to keep Britain in the EC.

The chosen strategy was re-negotiation of the terms of British entry to the EC, and Labour went to the polls in 1974 with a pledge to seek better terms than Heath had obtained and to pull out of the Community if these proved unobtainable. On the British list when discussions were broached in April were reform of the CAP, a reassessment of Britain's contribution to the EC budget, resistance to any undermining of Britain's regional policies by the EC, rejection of a fixed parity for sterling to fit in with suggestions from Brussels for Economic and Monetary Union, and readjustment of the Community's approach to trade with the Third World which would embrace more than France's ex-colonies. Though re-negotiation was in the hands of Callaghan, now Foreign Secretary, these demands were congenial to Wilson in that they would restore the balance in the EC in Britain's favour which he believed Heath had allowed the Community to skew. More than this, a hard line over re-negotiation would appease the anti-Europeans in the party while giving some comfort to the pro-Europeans.

Deep down, however, re-negotiation was a sham. No serious suggestion was made to undertake the impossible task of re-negotiating the Treaty of Rome, nor was the 1972 Treaty of Accession to be unravelled. The intention was rather to tinker with aspects of the latter. Moreover, the British re-negotiating team found itself not so much battering against a stone wall at Brussels as at an open door. This was not just because France and Germany were led by Helmut

Schmidt and Valery Giscard d'Estaing, who had a pragmatic approach to European cooperation and wanted to accommodate the British. As with Heath in the 1960s, negotiations took place on a 'moving belt', that is, with a Community which was continuing to develop. This time, though, the 'moving belt' favoured the Wilson Government, for many of the fundamentals on the British list became increasingly irrelevant as re-negotiation proceeded. Community discussions which were to produce the Lomé Convention in 1975 added a new dimension to trade between the EC and the developing countries, including the Commonwealth. The creation of an ERDF, and clear indications that Britain would be a chief claimant on the Fund, reduced fears of a conflict over policy in the regions. Moreover, a general increase in world food prices diverted resentment over the high cost of the CAP. At the same time, potentially troublesome progress towards EMU had disappeared almost to vanishing point because of the world economic recession. When, therefore, at a Community summit in Dublin in March 1975 an unwieldy formula was accepted which, though it did not reduce Britain's budget contribution, provided the prospect of future rebates, Wilson could claim victory. The same meeting also agreed upon advantageous terms of trade with the Community for New Zealand dairy produce over the next five years. All this was crucial for both party and domestic consumption, for 'the point of the exercise was to present the Prime Minister as a "St George" figure, who knew how to stand up to foreign dragons and would never sell his country short'; and his success was 'presented as an unequivocal acceptance of the British demands, a capitulation of the foreign dragons to the courage of the British champion' (George, 1990, p. 86).

The second stage of Wilson's strategy to preserve party and domestic unity was now brought into play. The electorate had been promised in 1974 that they would be consulted by a Labour Government when terms had been negotiated. Though it was not then clear how this might be done it soon became apparent that a single-issue General Election was too cumbersome and, with only a precarious majority in the Commons, too politically dangerous for Labour to contemplate. The possibility of a national referendum on Britain's entry into the EC had been mooted in Labour Party circles since defeat in the 1970 election but emerged as policy only slowly. This was, in part, due to the fact that it would be an innovatory constitutional experiment for Britain. It was the left of the party which embraced the idea first, in the spring of 1972 – Tony Benn appears to have been a key figure – largely because opinion polls indicated that a referendum would produce an anti-European result. Conversely, the right were opposed to a referendum – Roy Jenkins resigned from the Shadow Cabinet when it agreed to the idea in March. It was not until January 1975, however, that Wilson confirmed that a referendum would be held in the following summer. By then it could be claimed that re-negotiation had been successfully achieved. Moreover, public opinion had now begun to shift back in favour of Europe.

The referendum, held on 5 June, produced an overwhelming majority for continuation of British membership of the Community. It says something in itself that the European issue had produced so unique an experience in British history. Yet little else was novel. While the referendum gave legitimacy to Heath's move into Europe and Wilson's re-negotiation, it was essentially the approval of a confused and bored population voting for the *status quo* and taking their lead from the Government which, in March, had recommended them to do so. The wider issues of where a potentially federal Community might be heading and the implications of all this for Britain were swamped in arcane debates on farm subsidies and budget contributions. It is difficult to deny the view that,

> The most that could be said was that the issue was apparently settled, and a long-running conflict put to one side. More important for Wilson and his colleagues, it had been settled without bringing down the Labour government and by the adoption of a skilful mechanism which enabled the Labour Cabinet to continue in being despite the widest possible gulf between its members on such a key issue. Britain and the Wilson government had survived. The wider implications of Britain's relations with any kind of Europe, or the public's perception of them, were swept briskly to one side. (Morgan, 1990, p. 367)

Added to this, re-negotiation and the referendum inevitably broadcast negative signals over Britain's commitment to the EC. George Thomson, a pro-European member of Wilson's Shadow Cabinet who had resigned over the decision to hold a referendum, warned of having 'substantially run down our working capital of goodwill' in the Community between 1973 and 1975 (quoted in Childs, 1986, p. 253). Indeed, 'the British had over the years become faintly tiresome in the eyes of the continentals, what with their comings and goings and their insistence on renegotiating what had already been negotiated' (King, 1977, p. 135).

9

Reluctant Europeans, 1975—90

The Community to which the British had now, at last, seemed to commit themselves was an evolving organism rather than a static, fixed creation. The departure of de Gaulle from office in 1969 had not only helped open the door to British entry, it had also had a liberating effect on the EC itself. During the period of de Gaulle's domination, the basic objective of the Treaty of Rome, 'to lay the foundations of an ever-closer union among the peoples of Europe', had lain dormant. Attempts, in 1965, to link proposals for a Common Agricultural Policy (which de Gaulle wanted) to increased independence for both the European Parliament and the European Commission (which de Gaulle did not want) had produced a French boycott of the Council of Ministers. The outcome had been that whereas the CAP had moved forward, the drive to increase the supranationality of the Community had collapsed.

A summit meeting of the heads of government of the EC called by de Gaulle's successor, Georges Pompidou, at The Hague in 1969 demonstrated a change of atmosphere. The meeting inaugurated something like another *relance* of the European Idea, with agreement reached on the enlargement of the Community and proposals for Economic and Monetary Union. At the Paris summit of Community members in 1972, common action was embodied in a decision that such meetings be institutionalized as a European Council to meet regularly three times (later reduced to twice) a year. The goal of Economic and Monetary Union and, rather more vaguely, of European Union, was set for 1980. By 1974 the two issues which de Gaulle had vetoed, direct elections for the Parliament and an independent budget for the Commission, had been accepted. By this time too the Community had expanded to include Ireland and Denmark as well as Britain.

This new-found federalist fervour in Europe would almost certainly have presented problems for the British had it continued. Fortunately for Wilson and for Callaghan, who succeeded him as Prime Minister in March 1976, this did not last. The very decision to enlarge the Community by embracing less ardently supranational members such as Britain and Denmark was, in itself, a cause of a loss of impetus. Also, the always crucial Franco-German axis was now headed by individuals, Schmidt and Giscard, who were inclined to work towards more limited objectives for the Community. Most significantly, the oil crisis of the early 1970s meant that the rest of the decade was overshadowed by a world-wide economic recession which diverted attention from more radical schemes of union.

This dovetailed quite neatly with the British approach to the Community. As Prime Minister between 1975 and 1979, Callaghan was inclined to support American, rather than European, solutions to global economic problems. At the same time, her own particular, and severe, economic difficulties conspired to make Britain's attitude to European developments a matter of secondary importance. On top of high inflation and rising unemployment, Callaghan, in his first year in office, had to deal with a massive flight from sterling on the foreign exchange markets which reduced its value by over a quarter during his first year of government. Cuts in public expenditure made in an attempt to fend off the sterling crisis and which bit even deeper owing to the terms of a loan from the International Monetary Fund (IMF) angered the left of the Labour Party, which claimed that the Government had betrayed its most loyal supporters. To make matters more difficult, Callaghan headed a minority government which depended for its survival on the support of minority parties and especially the Liberals.

By mid-1978 monetary union was again on the Community agenda with Schmidt and Giscard putting forward the idea of a European Monetary System (EMS) as a new pathway towards EMU. According to Denis Healey, Callaghan's Chancellor of the Exchequer, their motive for this was that 'they saw it ... primarily in political terms, as leading to a European Monetary Union which would in turn lead to some sort of European integration across the board' (Healey, 1990, p. 438). This may have been so; though Schmidt, the main protagonist of EMS, seems to have been more concerned over the effect American proposals for combatting the world recession were having on Germany's currency. Washington's suggested way forward, that the stronger economies, like the German, should stimulate demand and thus help the weaker economies to expand, held the danger of inflation for these economies. But the policy which the US pursued in reality, allowing the value of the dollar to deteriorate, was causing a flight to the stronger Deutschmark and adding to the cost of German exports. Linking the European currencies together at a fixed rate of exchange – the heart of the EMS proposal – would have the advantage for Germany of reducing speculation against the Deutschmark because its value would be static. Also, the cost of German goods at a fixed currency might be more attractive than exports from the US costed on the basis of a fluctuating dollar. Finally, the EMS would provide a European lead to ending the recession, at initiative which, in Schmidt's eyes, seemed so badly lacking from the United States.

The system, which was functioning by 1979, allowed for two interlocking elements: an exchange rate mechanism (ERM) which would provide a common framework within which exchange rates could be adjusted to the benefit of internal European trade and its trade with the rest of the world; a European Currency Unit (ECU) which, enthusiasts suggested, should ultimately become the single currency of the Community. Again, to the dismay and irritation of many Europeans, the British decided to take what was at that time a unique position over the EMS, staying out of the ERM but participating in the pooling of currency reserves which backed the creation of the ECU. Labour's Chancellor, not in any case a convinced supporter of moves towards closer European cooperation, turned against the EMS after being convinced that it could serve only German interests, and at their partners' expense (Healey, 1990, p. 439). Callaghan's Atlanticist inclinations and his lukewarm stance towards the Community probably coloured his own final decision, though more specific economic and political considerations were also at play. While Schmidt saw the battle against the recession essentially in terms of a fight against inflation, with the EMS, in which each participating currency accepted the discipline of the system, playing a central role, Callaghan aligned himself with the American view that stimulation of growth was the key to economic upturn and that the stabilization of currencies was best achieved through an existing institution like the IMF. Underlying this thinking was Britain's particular trading position, the current economic difficulties which the British were facing and the fact that Britain's European partners 'were forming their "common market" out of the area that was their majority market anyway, whereas Britain's majority market lay elsewhere' (Porter, 1987, p. 125). The latter, an important factor in 1973, still applied five years on and Callaghan was reluctant to expose the pound to the rigour of being linked to the stronger Deutschmark – and within a Community with which Britain still did significantly less than half her trade (though this was increasing annually). Callaghan's half-way house seems, therefore, to have been a means of dousing his own apprehensions, addressing Britain's own economic concerns while, at the same time, giving some assurances of good intent to the Europeans.

Although this had the frequent drawback of compromise solutions, that of really pleasing no one, the British were by no means alone in putting domestic issues before the interests of the Community. The EMS itself, as Healey asserted, had been proposed by Schmidt as much to reduce pressure on the Deutschmark caused by a weak dollar as to lay the foundations for European Monetary Union. Giscard supported him for economic reasons which were essentially French (George, 1990, p. 127–8). When Greece, Portugal and Spain joined the EC in the 1980s all initially remained outside the ERM. Having said this, membership of the EMS was viewed as an indicator of a certain European *esprit de corps*. On a more general level, it also provides a good example of the way in which integration in the Community moves forward via an interplay of national and collective interests. In contrast, the British position over the EMS revealed something of Callaghan's standoffishness towards Europe and the old hankering for a more global approach to economic management. Whereas the French and Germans saw the EMS as a possible way out of the recession, he preferred to work with the Americans through the International Monetary Fund and shied away from full commitment to a European creation to which the United States was cool.

Callaghan also had still to tread warily with the left which, despite being outmanoeuvered by Wilson over Europe, continued to obstruct European developments whenever it could. It may be that the significant opposition to the EMS which was voiced by delegates to the Party Conference in October 1978 was a crucial factor in his decision that Britain would not participate fully. Undoubtedly it was party-political considerations which largely account for the fact that, uniquely amongst EC members, the Callaghan Government failed to meet the Community target for direct elections to the European Parliament. While the Prime Minister himself seems to have been willing to push forward with an obligation which he had inherited from Wilson that Britain, along with other EC members, should mount elections for the European Parliament which would replace government nominees by elected representatives, clearing the path towards this was hindered by the opponents of the EC in his party. Severe opposition to direct elections which, it was argued, would erode the political authority of Westminster emerged at the 1976 Party Conference. Though this failed to derail the Government's commitment to moving forward on the issue, fear of the domestic consequences of a party split meant that the necessary legislative preparations for elections to the European Parliament were delayed to the point where Britain might not be ready to participate in the innovatory procedure set for the spring of 1978. By the summer of 1977 it was clear that the only way to meet this date was to dispense with the creation of new European constituencies in the United Kingdom, and adopt instead a system of voting by some version of proportional representation. Callaghan − under pressure from the Liberals, his essential allies in the Commons − conceded. Proportional representation, however, was anathema to most MPs in both major parties who, though they wrapped their objections in constitutional terminology, were essentially fearful of its impact on the parliamentary landscape of Britain. A Cabinet revolt forced Callaghan to allow a free vote for Labour in the Commons debate on the new legislation for direct elections, which, combined with Conservative antipathy, effectively killed the proposal. The deadline could not now be met and, because of British foot-dragging, the process had to be postponed throughout the EC.

An even more seriously divisive problem resurfaced towards the end of Callaghan's government in the shape of Britain's contribution to the EC budget. This had been a key issue in Wilson's re-negotiation of the terms of entry but it had never been effectively settled, and now as the end of the transitional arrangements aimed at gradually integrating Britain into the budgetary system came within sight − this was to occur in 1980 − the view gained momentum in Britain that the British contribution was excessive. It was possible to argue this in a double sense. First of all, because of the formula devised during the 1970s to give the Community financial independence, Britain would be contributing more than some of her partners whose economic strength was greater than her own. Britain continued significantly to import goods, particularly food, from outside the EC. Yet the Community budget was made up of tariffs on such imports − plus 1 per cent of each member's receipts from value added tax (VAT). Added to this, Britain received less back from the budget than other member states. At the heart of the issue was the CAP. This ate up around two-thirds of the Community budget in the late 1970s and was growing to a point at which bankruptcy loomed. At the same time, because of her lower agricultural base compared to others in the EC and because the CAP left so little to other means of disbursement such as the ERDF, returns from the budget trickled, rather than flowed, back to Britain.

From their own point of view, the British case seemed a sound one and the Callaghan Government was determined to fight its corner, giving notice during the winter of 1978 of its intention to readjust the balance. To the majority in the EC, however, it looked more like special pleading on the part of a member who refused to adjust to new circumstances by shifting its trading base, exhibited a lack of Community spirit and seemed intent again on opening the whole process of re-negotiation because the rules, which she had accepted on entry, did not suit. The matter was made the more intractable because of the British insistence on linking the budget question to the CAP; for, while majority opinion in Britain might condemn its excesses, to the Community as a whole it was 'an almost holy object . . . and criticisms about it tended to be dismissed almost as statements of heresy' (Urwin, 1991, p. 186).

It was left to the Government of Margaret Thatcher, which was elected in 1979, to take up the cudgels over budget reform. This was done with a stridency which soon became a hallmark of both her domestic and her European policies. In this case, the two were linked. As the head of a Government committed to reductions in public spending there was a consistency in her demands that Britain's membership of the Community should cost less. A struggle against Brussels, always a popular target at home because of its reputation as the epitome of bureaucratic meddling and waste, was also useful in raising Britain's international profile and in reinforcing the Prime Minister's image as a formidable fighter for her convictions. There was also Thatcher's temperamental inclination towards conflict which appears to have been accentuated by Schmidt's and Giscard's misconceived attempts to treat her as an inferior newcomer.

The style was set early on, with the notorious demand made at the Dublin European Council in November 1979 for our 'own money back'. At first Thatcher seemed satisfied to entertain offers of cash rebates, but wrangling over the amount and the uncertainty that

108

refunds would be available annually had, within the year, hardened her position into a determination to achieve a permanent solution through a restructuring of the Community budget. Thatcher's campaign was aided by the looming insolvency of the Community itself, for which the costs of the CAP were principally to blame. The answer was seen to lie in an increase in the 1 per cent of VAT receipts from the member states, but British approval for this was essential. Their negotiating advantage was exploited to the full when, in May 1982, the British vetoed agreement on agricultural price levels for the coming year − a necessary preliminary for implementing the CAP − insisting on a final resolution of the budget question as the price for the ending of this intransigence. By this time, Britain was engaged in a two-front struggle with her EC partners: in the short term, to gain acceptable annual repayments; and in the long term, for more radical budget reform which would be to her advantage.

It turned out to be remarkably successful. Between 1980 and 1983 Britain, through hard bargaining, received a substantial series of rebates. By the time the European Council met at Stuttgart in the summer of 1983 there was a general recognition that some permanent solution to the budgetary issue was required and that this must entail some modification of the CAP. Having said this, Thatcher's abrasive tone had an alienating effect, causing voices to be raised suggesting that the Community might be better off without Britain and that a two-speed route to union, with Britain in the slow lane, might be to everyone's advantage. But this was not what Britain wanted. It was not so much that Thatcher 'was an agnostic rather than a believer' on Europe (Morgan, 1990, p. 454). Rather, she took a neo-Gaullist view, hoping to extend her domestic policy of freeing restrictions to enterprise while rigorously maintaining national authority and identity. This combination of a British determination to remain a central participant in the Community and the Community's desire to thwart looming bankruptcy laid the foundation for an acceptable compromise.

Though the British case was narrowly self-interested and presented in a manner calculated to irritate, it was made the more persuasive to many because of the expansion of the EC to include Greece (1981), Spain (1986) and Portugal (1986), which suggested that changes in budgetary contributions and in the CAP were necessary for the good of the Community as a whole. By 1984 a small step towards reform of the CAP had been made by an agreement to reduce milk production in the EC and modestly to pare down agricultural subsidies. From

109

now on, 'Britain was no longer isolated in the role of demander but merely one of a number of states which recognized there was a problem but could not find a solution' (Allen, 1988, p. 42).

This change of climate and Britain's ability to claim that the defects of the CAP were now being tackled paved the way for a settlement of the budget dispute at a meeting of the European Council at Fontainebleau in the summer of 1984. In exchange for agreeing to a Community-wide hike in VAT contributions to Brussels, Britain obtained an annual rebate of 66 per cent of the difference between her VAT contributions and the amount she received from EC funding. Stephen George has pointed out that this was not achieved without some concessions on the part of the British over how budget contributions were calculated and that agreement might have been reached on marginally more favourable terms three months earlier at the Brussels European Council in March had Thatcher's negotiating techniques been more sophisticated (George, 1990, pp. 155–8). Fontainebleau was, nevertheless, presented as a triumph for the British position and it was possible to view it as a 'watershed in the Conservative government's relations with its Community partners' (Allen, 1988, p. 41).

Many were indeed inclined to accept that the conflict over the budget was no more than a means of reversing the disadvantages of Britain's late entry to the Community, a continuation of the process begun by Wilson and Callaghan, and that it 'simply reflected the government's attempts to effect changes in the EC's internal economic and political arrangements that would enable Britain to play a role in intra-community affairs rather more commensurate with its status as a Great Power' (Sanders, 1990, p. 160). In a sense, the British could now be seen to have 'come of age' as members of the EC in learning to trade off their own interests against those of the wider Community. This was something that the original Six had become adept at over the years and it has been argued that

> Britain under Mrs. Thatcher's first administration was neither fundamentally more 'pro' or 'anti' the European Community than most of its other members. Like them, it defended its national interests within an increasingly confederal framework. This may not have been the intention of the founders of the Common Market but then life goes on and democratic institutions alter to reflect the needs and wishes of changing electorates. (Sked and Cook, 1990, p. 381)

The fluctuating demands and desires of electorates, of course, presuppose the desirability of an informed public opinion educated, in this context, in the implications of what developing collaboration with Europe would mean to Britain. In common with all its predecessors since 1945, however, the Thatcher Government failed to provide the basis for reasoned and balanced debate. On the contrary, Thatcher went 'out of her way to cultivate the impression of her constant struggle with our European partners to safeguard Britain's interests' (Allen, 1988, p. 52).

Nevertheless, there were indications that, under Thatcher, Britain might be becoming more *communautaire*. Despite her marked preference to restore the Anglo-American transatlantic circle in British foreign policy, Hugo Young's assertion that 'winning the battle over Britain's contribution to the Community budget did not herald a new era of Euro-minded leadership. The country remained hooked on its special relationship with the United States, and a combative relationship all points east of Dover' is not entirely fair (Hugo Young, 1989, p. 249). Her admiration for President Reagan and the affinities between his and her own views on economic policy and East–West relations did not prevent her from taking a line in foreign affairs which sometimes cut across the Anglo-American partnership and tended to emphasize Britain's solidarity with Europe. This was the case over American insistence in 1982 that the Western Europeans pull out of the scheme to have natural gas piped to them from Siberia and the dismay at the Reagan-Gorbachev arms-control agreement reached at Reykjavik in 1986 without consultation with America's European allies.

Moreover, though little had been done, following the failure of the EDC in the 1950s, to coordinate the defence and foreign policies of members of the Community, a process of European Political Cooperation (EPC) had emerged in 1970 which allowed for detailed discussion between the European states prior to any significant shift in their foreign policies. In 1981 an initiative by the Thatcher Government helped firm up EPC by an agreement on compulsory consultation following any international crisis. Less positively, Thatcher's acquiescence in the deployment of cruise missiles in Britain and in the use of US planes from bases in Britain to bomb Libya in 1986 provided high-profile examples of her attachment to the Atlantic link. Her insistence that no new European institutions should get in the way of this, plus her aversion to anything which might erode national sovereignty, meant that Britain's earlier initiatives over EPC were not followed through 'and the British government's determination to pursue a very public "independent" line ensured that even this coordination was severely limited' (Sanders, 1990, p. 165).

For a while after the European Council at Fontainebleau it looked as though things might be different. Not only had the most serious point of irritation between Britain and the EC, the budget, been largely cleared away and in a manner that seemed to balance British interests with those of the larger Community, the British surprised their partners by presenting to the Council a discussion paper, called 'Europe – The Future', which laid out proposals for the completion of a truly free internal market by the dismantling of all obstacles to commerce. This was to be the germ of the Single European Act (SEA) agreed at the Luxembourg European Council in December 1985. The objective of a fully economically integrated Europe was still hampered by currency regulations, trading standards and impediments to the free movement of capital and labour. The SEA was intended to remove these obstacles by the end of 1992. But the British had not become sudden converts to federalism. On the contrary, the intention rather was to divert the rebirth of enthusiasm on the Continent for political integration and institutional reform along lines which Britain could tolerate, and to do so before this fervour left Britain on the sidelines again. As was soon to become quite evident, Thatcher's aggressive stance on European issues was neither temporary nor merely a bargaining technique but a permanent style which sprang from a fundamental suspicion of the intentions of the Europeans. In the long run, it was to be a crucial flaw which damaged Britain's relations with her European partners, possibly inspired them to more radical federalist programmes than most would have otherwise entertained and was ultimately fatal to the Thatcher Government itself.

Arguably, Margaret Thatcher was unlucky in that her Premiership coincided with another in a series of periodic spurts of enthusiasm within the EC which pushed Europe further towards integration. In this case, it amounted to a *relance* comparable to those which had taken place in the mid-1950s and late 1960s. While Thatcher's distaste for European union was no more profound than that of Wilson and Callaghan (though the tone in which it was expressed was more shrill), it was thrown into negative relief by the visionary statements emerging from the Continent in a way which theirs never was. As usual, the resurgence of federalism sprang from a mixture of practical and emotional considerations. The Genscher-Colombo Plan of 1981 (named after its authors, the Foreign Ministers of West

Germany and Italy) proposed political unification as a means of competing with the Japanese and with a revived American economy. On the other hand, a Draft Treaty on European Union taken up by the European Parliament in 1984 was founded on the idealism of the Italian federalist Altiero Spinelli. It was not easy to decelerate this momentum. At Fontainebleau, the Dooge Committee, named after its Irish chairman, was set up to investigate institutional reform. When it reported in March 1985 it recommended a more effective role for the European Parliament and the end of the national veto in Community decision-making. Coincidentally, the new President of the European Commission, Jacques Delors, was arguing that if a genuine single market was, at last, to be achieved there would have to be an increase in supranationalism in order to override those national economic interests which had delayed the process in the past. This, in turn, would require institutional change and amendments to the Treaty of Rome.

This was most unwelcome to the British, who felt that moves towards a deregulated market were perfectly possible without radical institutional change. More particularly, they resisted the call for an inter-governmental conference (IGC), a constitutional necessity before any alterations to the Treaty of Rome could be made, for fear that this might lead to even further demands for reform. Though Britain was outvoted on this question at the Milan summit of June 1985, the IGC did not justify these apprehensions. This had much to do with a recognition on the part of the British that if they wanted the 'Thatcherization' of Europe to take place at all then they must lean moderately towards the views of their partners and thereby defuse the more assertive supranationalist demands. This provided the climate for the agreement at the Luxembourg European Council in December to create a single integrated market within the EC by the end of 1992, one of the most significant developments in European integration since 1957. Proposals for institutional reform at Luxembourg were pared down to the minimum, with only a limited extension of majority voting and only a modest extension of the powers of the European Parliament. In exchange, Britain accepted that the objective of a free market by 1992 would require a revision of the Treaty of Rome and was prepared to go along with what appeared to be innocuous statements on eventual European unity and the development of the EMS. In other words, 'at the end of 1985 the Community seemed to be embarked on a course very similar to that desired by Britain' (George, 1990, p. 185).

But this apparent victory for British pragmatism was a mirage; and Margaret Thatcher may have been among the first to sense this. According to Stephen George, the achievement of the Single European Act provides an example of 'successful diplomatic manoeuvring, involving Britain in gaining more than it conceded. [It does] not add up to the behaviour of an awkward partner, but to that of a normal and skilful actor in the Community game.' It was, he argues, Thatcher's subsequent confrontations and outspokenness which vexed her European colleagues and even 'seemed to push the Christian Democratic leaders of West Germany and the Benelux states into reopening the question of institutional reform which had apparently been resolved in a manner not unfavourable to Britain in 1985' (George, 1990, pp. 206–7). That Thatcher ultimately induced her own downfall partly because of her stance on Europe is difficult to deny, and George's suggestion that she was outmanoeuvred by her opponents in Europe is supported by the circumstances surrounding her fall from power. But her basic error perhaps lay in the Luxembourg agreement itself, the consequences of which she soon realized and attempted to escape from.

The question of institutional reform had not, in fact, been finally settled at Luxembourg. Although the Single European Act gave comfort both to those who wished to see greater political union and those who did not, the virtual eradication of frontier controls, the opening of markets, the free movement of labour and financial services and the harmonization of taxes each tipped the scales emphatically in favour of the argument for new European institutions to manage such changes which, in turn, implied a further erosion of national sovereignty. By the summer of 1988 such implications had taken solid shape in firm proposals for the creation of a European Central Bank and the transformation of the ECU into the single currency of the Community. This was viewed by Thatcher as an invitation to Britain to surrender its economic policy and thus its very sovereignty, and the bank was dismissed as not to be considered – 'in my lifetime, nor, if I'm twanging a harp, for quite a long time afterwards' (quoted in Reynolds, 1991, p. 271). At the same time, she rejected full British participation in the exchange rate mechanism of the EMS, a necessary preliminary to monetary union.

Delors was in full agreement with Thatcher's predictions on reductions of national sovereignty, though he did not share her alarm and went out of his way to assert to the European Parliament, in July 1988, that given ten years, 80 per cent of economic, financial and social legislation was likely to be directed from Brussels. Worse still

114

(so far as the British Prime Minister was concerned), at a meeting with the British TUC in September Delors insisted that 1992 was not just about eliminating frontiers but about providing better conditions for people at home and at work. Thatcher's response came some days later at a speech to the College of Europe in Bruges in which she denounced the notion of a 'European superstate' and condemned Delors' views as creeping, back-door socialism. Moreover, her expressed fears over problems of drugs and terrorists put the very question of abolishing frontier controls, the heart of the Luxembourg agreement itself, in doubt.

Bruges may well have been a turning point. The non-socialist leaders of West Germany, Belgium, Holland and Luxembourg were quick to associate themselves with Delors' views. Stephen George suggests that

> In her Bruges speech Thatcher had appeared to repudiate the commitment in the Single European Act to a European union, presenting instead the neo-Gaullist idea of a Europe of independent states which would cooperate closely but not submit to any central control over economic policy, nor move to any sort of political union. Now the Christian Democratic Prime Ministers counter-attacked by implicitly repudiating the Single European Act themselves in favour of a more far-reaching amendment to the treaties. (George, 1990, p. 195)

If this was the case it was only a further shove to a bandwagon which was already moving, and the Prime Minister found herself increasingly attempting to reverse the irreversible. On the litmus test of monetary union Thatcher found herself steadily having to concede defeat. At the Madrid European Council in June 1989, isolated in a minority of one and pressed by her own Chancellor and Foreign Secretary, she was forced to accept eventual full British entry to the EMS – though this was hedged by strict conditions and, unlike her partners, she refused to view this as part of a process leading to a Central Bank and a single currency. The *Financial Times* was moved to warn that 'after 40 years of experience, it should be burnt into the consciousness of a British Prime Minister that she may slow down an evolution on which all other members of the EC are resolved; she may influence its form; but she will not stop it' (23 June 1989).

By this time, the European question had begun to have alarming repercussions at home. The Conservatives did badly in the elections for the European Parliament which were held in the same month as

115

the Madrid summit, an apparent rejection by the electorate of the negative message in their campaign. An earlier indication that public opinion did not necessarily share Thatcher's European attitudes had been given during the Westland affair in 1986. Here the Government's decision to back an American takeover of the Westland helicopter company rather than support a bid from a European consortium as the Defence Secretary, Michael Heseltine, wished, did not find popular backing; and Heseltine's resignation over the issue was the first departure from Thatcher's Cabinet related to the Government's commitment to Europe. More were to follow.

In October 1989 Nigel Lawson, the Chancellor of the Exchequer, resigned because of the Prime Minister's resistance to joining the exchange rate mechanism of the EMS, a position which he claimed was fuelling rather than fighting inflation. Indiscretions in an interview in which monetary union was referred to as 'a German racket designed to take over the whole of Europe', the French as the 'poodles' of the Germans and the EC Commissioners as 'unelected, reject politicians' forced Nicholas Ridley, the Trade and Industry Secretary, to resign in July 1990. This time, though, the received view was that Ridley had spoken aloud the Prime Minister's private thoughts. Four months later it was the turn of Geoffrey Howe. Howe had lost his job as Foreign Secretary for his part, along with Lawson, in pushing Thatcher into a reluctant commitment to full EMS membership at the Madrid summit. To the surprise of most, Britain did join the ERM in October, but this was essentially part of the domestic campaign against inflation and was timed to wrong-foot the Labour Party at the end of their annual Party Conference and at a time when a General Election seemed to loom. It did not mark any significant change in policy towards Europe. This was clearly demonstrated by angry out-bursts from the Prime Minister against monetary union during and after a European Council in Rome in November which triggered Howe's resignation. With a devastating resignation speech — in which he rejected the Thatcher vision of a 'continent that is positively teeming with ill-intentioned people, scheming, in her words, to extinguish democracy, to "dissolve our national identities", to lead us "through the back door into a federal Europe"' — Howe precipitated a leadership challenge in the Conservative Party which, in November 1990, Margaret Thatcher lost.

It was an astonishing turn of events. Although critical of her 'uniquely bleak vision of Europe', *The Independent* noted that 'the leadership election is not about Europe. It is about Mrs. Thatcher.

116

She is the issue' (8 November 1990). This was true. The contest was fought essentially because she had become highly unpopular in the country and was likely to be a liability in the approaching General Election. In turn, this unpopularity had more to do with domestic issues such as unprecedentedly high interest rates and the imposition of the Poll Tax than with squabbles with Europeans. Nevertheless, Europe had provided not only the circumstance which dislodged her – once again, her European colleagues appear to have deliberately accelerated the programme for EMU at Rome as a means of isolating her – it also remained a central issue in the leadership campaign. For the first time in post-war history the European question had played a central part in bringing down a British government.

The party coup which removed Thatcher indicated a deep rift over Europe within the British governing elite. The pro-Europeans were able to gain the ascendency not because they were radical proponents of full integration – there were few of these in the anti-Thatcher camp of the Tory party – but because they could point to the damaging effect which the Prime Minister's antipathy had already had the domestic economy and the further dangers inherent in Britain lagging behind a Community which seemed determined to move forward. This was also how the British electorate had come to see it.

This change in popular mood had been a relatively recent development. At the start of the Thatcher years her battles for budgetary reform tapped the resentment against a Community which seemed to have cost people dear and offered little in return other than petty harmonization regulations. But, just as the Community itself had become indissolubly interlocked through a gradual process of learning to work together, so the British seemed to have reconciled themselves to viewing their future as bound to Europe's. One basic imperative for joining the Community in the first place had failed to produce the desired result, and 'membership of the EC had done nothing to arrest [Britain's] decline in economic performance' (Reynolds, 1991, p. 274). Yet, direct experience of the ways of life of their partners through increased holiday and business travel tended to suggest that the higher living standards which most Western Europeans enjoyed might rub off on the British if they stuck with them. The campaign to prepare for 1992 which got under way in Britain, belatedly, at the end of 1980s probably reinforced a growing acceptance that, to coin a Thatcherite phrase, 'there is no alternative.' Even the Labour Party came to recognize this in 1988 when it abandoned its commitment to take Britain out of the EC if returned to power, though it had not yet

117

rediscovered Ernest Bevin's European vision and remained hardly less sceptical than the Government over EMU.

Oddly, the 'populist' Margaret Thatcher remained insensitive to these shifts. Her carping criticisms of Europe seemed *passé* and may even have been counter-productive, given her developing personal unpopularity. The same applied to her preference for a restoration of a 'special relationship' with the United States which was also undermined by a distaste for the stridency of American external affairs discernible in the late 1980s. Even her attitude to the dramatic collapse of authoritarian government in Eastern Europe during 1989, which she claimed to have helped produce, seemed old-fashioned and was viewed, through her eyes, not as the beginning of a new chapter in European integration perhaps embracing the East, but rather as an excuse to put the brakes on deepening economic and monetary union in the West on the ground that it would prevent the widening of Europe to embrace the East. This did not mean that the British people had opted to embrace federalism. Few associated the EC with the ideals of Monnet and Schuman, principally because they had rarely been asked to do so by political leaders who, for the most part, had become pro-European by circumstance rather than by conviction. Understandably, therefore, polls continued to demonstrate a schizophrenic response to integration (*Independent on Sunday*, 4 November 1990; *Guardian*, 14 December 1990). Though a reduction in the authority of Westminster and the replacement of the pound coin with the ECU were viewed with little relish, a majority, none the less, seemed able to accept that they would fare no worse if Britain's economic policy were to be directed from Brussels. The signs were that, although the fundamental political and constitutional changes which were bound to follow greater economic and monetary integration had not yet been fully grasped, the British people were prepared to view their status as members of a wider European community more positively and with less apprehension than they once did.

10

Conclusion

The story of Britain's move towards Europe is an unfinished one. In the first place, our full understanding of why two successive governments of differing political complexions changed the thrust of British policy and decided to apply to enter the EC remains incomplete. The availability of official records under the thirty-year rule has offered new insights into why those who made British policy in the first twenty years or so after the Second World War acted in the way they did. However, the lack of such material for the later period which prohibits detailed judgements on the significance of the advice of the Treasury and the Foreign Office, and other political and economic pressures, necessarily implies a less well-rounded picture. It may be that this hidden documentation, in the end, tells us nothing fundamentally new, though the information we now have on Ernest Bevin's 'Grand Design' and his Euro-Africa policy and on Anthony Eden's attitude to Europe suggests otherwise.

Added to this, the process of Britain's developing relationship with Europe is an ongoing one. While we may not yet be in a position to give a final verdict on precisely why British policy changed from the early sixties onwards, the essentially practical motives for this shift are clear. This pragmatism, with its emphasis on the economic and political advantages of membership for Britain, ignored the fact that Britain had bound herself by the Treaty of Rome to a potentially federalist Community. No government since Macmillan's, including that of the pro-European Heath, felt it necessary to inform the British electorate of the full implications of this. Instead, they preferred to adopt a more or less confrontational stance within a Community to which, it was asserted, nothing significant had been surrendered.

This mattered less when federalist feeling in Europe was relatively subdued, as it was throughout much of the 1970s when Britain entered the EC. Once it was in the ascendency again, during the 1980s, the thrust towards fuller integration proved problematical to the British Government. It may be that the end of the Thatcher Government will come to be seen as a turning-point. Clearly the Prime Minister was dropped because, among other things, her Little Englander style was out of step with a public which had virtually taught itself that, come what may, Britain's future lay in a more tightly bonded Europe. A sense was emerging, as Hugo Young put it, that 'the integrationist thrust ... is the likely long-term course of history. It has, with stops and starts, been the thrust of the last 20 years. The prophets of impasse have proved false, the prophets of evolution correct' (*The Guardian*, 10 September 1991). Almost simultaneously, the parochialism of British reluctance to immerse themselves more fully in Europe was thrown into dramatic relief by the collapse of communism, first in Eastern Europe and then in the Soviet Union itself. This has provided an extraordinary new twist to the history of integration. The possibility exists that by the end of the 1990s the Community of Twelve will have doubled in size, taking in states up to the frontiers of the former USSR.

Having said this, the impact of these changes upon British policy-makers remains unclear. Thatcher's replacement, John Major, though he jettisoned the Thatcher style, did not relinquish her preference for loose inter-governmental cooperation between the EC states and caution towards monetary union. Nor was the European stance of the Labour Party strikingly different. It may well be that, after all, a familiar pattern is retained and that, by the end of this century, Britain will continue to be the awkward partner on the fringes of a politically and economically united Europe.

References

Acheson, D. G. 1969: *Present at the Creation*, New York: Norton.
Adamthwaite, Anthony 1985: Britain and the world, 1945–49: the view from the 'Foreign Office'. *International Affairs*, 61/2, 223–35.
Adamthwaite, Anthony 1988: The Foreign Office and policy making. In J. W. Young (ed.), *The Foreign Policy of Churchill's Peacetime Administration 1951–55*. Leicester: University Leicester Press, 1–28.
Allen, David 1988: British foreign policy and West European cooperation. In Peter Byrd (ed.), *British Foreign Policy Under Thatcher*. Oxford: Philip Allan, 40–54.
Barnet, R. J. 1984: *Allies: America, Europe and Japan Since the War*. London: Cape.
Bartlett, C. J. 1977: *A History of Postwar Britain 1945–74*. London: Longman.
Bartlett, C. J. 1989: *British Foreign Policy in the Twentieth Century*. London: Macmillan.
Boyce, Robert 1989: British capitalism and the idea of European unity between the Wars. In P. M. R. Stirk (ed.), *European Unity in Context: the Interwar Period*. London: Pinter, 65–83.
Bullen, R. (ed.) 1986: *Documents on British Policy Overseas Series II*, vol. I. London: HMSO.
Bullock, Alan 1983: *Ernest Bevin: Foreign Secretary*. London: Heinemann.
Cairncross, Alec 1985: *Years of Recovery: British Economic Policy 1945–51*. London: Methuen.
Camps, Miriam 1964: *Britain and the European Community 1955–63*. Oxford: Oxford University Press.
Carlton, David 1986: *Anthony Eden*. London: Allen and Unwin.
Charlton, Michael 1983: *The Price of Victory*. London: BBC.
Childs, David 1986: *Britain Since 1945*. London: Routledge.
Dockrill, Saki 1989: Britain and the settlement of the West German rearmament question in 1954. In M. Dockrill and J. W. Young (eds), *British Foreign Policy 1945–56*. London: Macmillan, 149–72.

Edmonds, R. 1986: *Setting the Mould: the United States and Britain 1945–50.* Oxford: Oxford University Press.

Fursdon, Edward 1980: *The European Defence Community: A History.* London: Macmillan.

George, Stephen 1990: *An Awkward Partner: Britain in the European Community.* Oxford: Oxford University Press.

George-Brown, Lord 1972: *In My Way.* Harmondsworth: Penguin.

Greenwood, Sean 1983: Return to Dunkirk: the origins of the Anglo-French Treaty of March 1947. *Journal of Strategic Studies,* 6, 49–65.

Greenwood, Sean 1984: Ernest Bevin, France and 'Western Union' August 1945–February 1946. *European History Quarterly,* 14, 319–37.

Greenwood, Sean 1986: Bevin, the Ruhr and the division of Germany: August 1945–December 1946. *Historical Journal,* 29, 203–12.

Healey, Denis 1990: *The Time of My Life.* Harmondsworth: Penguin.

Hogan, Michael J. 1989: *The Marshall Plan: America, Britain and the Reconstruction of Western Europe, 1947–52.* Cambridge: Cambridge University Press.

Horne, Alistair 1989: *Macmillan 1957–86.* London: Macmillan.

Kent, John 1989: Bevin's imperialism and the idea of Euro-Africa 1945–49. In M. Dockrill and J. W. Young (eds), *British Foreign Policy 1945–56.* London: Macmillan, 47–76.

King, Anthony 1977: *Britain Says Yes: the 1975 Referendum on the Common Market.* Washington, DC: American Enterprise Institute.

Kitzinger, U. 1973: *Diplomacy and Persuasion: How Britain Joined the Common Market.* London: Thames and Hudson.

Kruger, Peter 1989: European ideology and European reality: European unity and German foreign policy in the 1920s. In P. M. R. Stirk (ed.), *European Unity in Context: the Interwar Period.* London: Pinter, 84–98.

Lamb, R. 1987: *The Failure of the Eden Government.* London: Sidgwick and Jackson.

Loth, Wilfried 1988: *The Division of the World 1941–55.* London: Routledge.

McDougall, W. A. 1979: Political economy versus national sovereignty: French structures for German economic integration after Versailles. *Journal of Modern History,* 51, 4–23.

Manderson-Jones, R. B. 1972: *The Special Relationship: Anglo-American Relations and Western European Unity 1947–56.* London: Weidenfeld and Nicolson.

Milward, Alan S. 1987: *The Reconstruction of Western Europe 1945–51.* London: Methuen.

Morgan, K. O. 1990: *The People's Peace: British History 1945–89.* Oxford: Oxford University Press.

Mowat, R. C. 1973: *Creating the European Community.* London: Blandford Press.

Northedge, F. S. 1974: *Descent From Power: British Foreign Policy 1945–73.* London: Allen and Unwin.

Porter, B. 1987: *Britain, Europe and the World 1850–1986: Delusions of Grandeur*. London: Allen and Unwin.

Rappaport, A. 1981: The United States and European integration: the first phase. *Diplomatic History*, 5/2, 121–49.

Reynolds, David 1991: *Britannia Overruled*. London: Longman.

Rhodes James, R. 1986: *Anthony Eden*. London: Weidenfeld and Nicolson.

Robbins, Keith 1983: *The Eclipse of a Great Power: Modern Britain 1870–1975*. London: Longman.

Rothwell, V. 1982: *Britain and the Cold War 1941–47*. London: Cape.

Sanders, D. 1990: *Losing an Empire, Finding a Role: British Foreign Policy Since 1945*. London: Macmillan.

Shlaim, Avi 1978: *Britain and the Origins of European Unity 1940–51*. Reading: University of Reading Press.

Shlaim, A., Jones, P. and Sainsbury, K. 1977: *British Foreign Secretaries Since 1945*. London: David and Charles.

Sked, A. and Cook, C. 1990: *Post-War Britain: A Political History*. Harmondsworth: Penguin.

Stirk, P. M. R. 1989: Crisis and continuity in interwar Europe. In P. M. R. Stirk (ed.), *European Unity in Context: the Interwar Period*. London: Pinter, 1–22.

Trachtenberg, M. 1980: *Reparation in World Politics: France and European Economic Diplomacy 1916–23*. New York: Columbia University Press.

Urwin, D. W. 1989: *Western Europe Since 1945: A Political History*. London: Longman.

Urwin, D. W. 1991: *The Community of Europe*. London: Longman.

Warner, G. 1984: The Labour Governments and the unity of Western Europe 1945–51. In R. Ovendale (ed.), *The Foreign Policy of the British Labour Governments 1945–51*. Leicester: University of Leicester Press, 61–82.

Warner, G. 1989: The Anglo-American special relationship. *Diplomatic History*, 13, 479–99.

Willis, F. Roy 1968: *France, Germany and the New Europe 1945–1967*. Oxford: Oxford University Press.

Young, Hugo 1989: *One of Us*. London: Macmillan.

Young, J. W. 1984: *Britain, France and the Unity of Europe 1945–51*. Leicester: University of Leicester Press.

Young, J. W. 1985: Churchill's 'No' to Europe: the 'rejection' of European Union by Churchill's post-war government, 1951–52. *Historical Journal*, 28, 923–37.

Young, J. W. 1988a: German rearmament and the European Defence Community. In J. W. Young (ed.), *The Foreign Policy of Churchill's Peacetime Administration 1951–55*. Leicester: University of Leicester Press, 81–108.

Young, J. W. 1988b: The Schuman Plan and British association. In J. W. Young (ed.), *The Foreign Policy of Churchill's Peacetime Administration 1951–55*. Leicester: University of Leicester Press, 109–34.

Young, J. W. 1989: 'The parting of the ways?' Britain, the Messina Conference and the Spaak Committee, June–December 1955. In M. Dockrill and J. W. Young (eds), *British Foreign Policy 1945–56*. London: Macmillan, 197–224.

Index